So
Heart
and
Mind
Can
Fill

# So
# Heart
# and
# Mind
# Can
# Fill

Reflections
for
Living

Lou Guntzelman

Saint Mary's Press
Christian Brothers Publications
Winona, Minnesota

In memory of those two
who brought me to the feast of life,
my parents,
Eleonora and Lou

The author wishes to thank those who supported and helped in this writing endeavor, especially *EastSide Weekend* editor Susan McHugh for the weekly opportunity in her paper, and Carol Fibbe and Bev Williamson for their many hours of proofing, typing, editing, and offering insightful suggestions.

Genuine recycled paper with 10% post-consumer waste.
Printed with soy-based ink.

The publishing team included Michael Wilt, development editor; David Thorstad, copy editor; Barbara Bartelson, production editor and typesetter; Maurine R. Twait, art director and cover designer; David R. Twait, cover photo; Karen Kryzsko, cover pottery; pre-press, printing, and binding by the graphics division of Saint Mary's Press.

The acknowledgments continue on page 131.

Printed in the United States of America

Printing: 9 8 7 6 5 4 3 2

Year: 2006 05 04 03 02 01 00 99

ISBN 0-88489-523-8

# Contents

# Introduction

EXPERIENCE AND REFLECTION can produce wisdom. When wisdom solidifies it often finds expression in the form of succinct proverbs. So it was with my grandmother. Many children, many years of hard work, and her penchant for prayer and reflection helped her develop a gentle wisdom and a sparkling eye. Her reflections often produced insightful proverbs that hit the mark and opened eyes. On one occasion, when she noticed one of her sons floating dreamily on clouds of infatuation about a new love, she first rejoiced with him and remarked that the young lady was, indeed, a very attractive person. Yet, knowing that a lot more time and understanding were needed before any important decisions could be made, she pointed to an hourglass with all the sand in the bottom. She lovingly remarked, "When the heart fills, the mind empties." She then urged much time, talk, and reflection so both heart and mind could fill.

When feeling is supreme, then the only standards by which we can judge the worth of an experience, an idea, or a behavior are its pleasurableness, pragmatism, and intensity. We consider something true because emotion—not reason—says so. Yet emotions alone are an unreliable foundation on which to build a life, a belief system, a spirituality.

We live in an era when people feel strongly about many issues, but an era that does not encourage much solid reflection and study. Someone has coined the term *sheeple* for those people who act like sheep, just following along, feeding on short sound bites, bumper stickers, slogans, and self-interested conclusions concerning the deeper issues of life. We nibble at the top of complex matters and move on, thinking we're well fed and well informed.

In *The Road Less Traveled and Beyond,* psychiatrist M. Scott Peck asks:

> How often, in fact, do we stop to think about what we believe? One of the major dilemmas we face both as individuals and as a society is simplistic thinking—or the failure to think at all. It isn't just a problem, it is *the* problem.
>
> Given the imperfections of our society and the apparent downward spiral of spiritual and moral values in recent years, thinking has become a grave issue . . . because it is the means by which we consider, decide, and act upon everything in our increasingly complex world.

This book of essays is an invitation to think, to reflect. These essays were previously published as weekly columns in *EastSide Weekend,* a secular neighborhood newspaper in Cincinnati, Ohio. They were written for the general public, of any denomination or none. Their purpose is not to serve as answers but as catalysts to deeper, thoughtful examination of various life issues and situations. They are of a spiritual, psychological nature, written in ordinary language for the ordinary person. Whatever the topic—heroes and celebrities, loneliness, cleverness versus justice, or the joys of heaven—each essay is meant to stimulate further thought, reading, or discussion. They will, I hope, whet the appetite of the reader to obtain deeper insight.

Perhaps I should have written at the conclusion of each essay, "What do you really *think* about this matter, and what process of thought or reason—not just feeling—leads you to that conclusion?" Sometimes we're stymied by such a question because we discover that what we think is determined only by what we feel, without the benefit of facts, logic, or principles.

*So Heart and Mind Can Fill* is written to intrigue minds first, then flow down into the heart.

## PART ONE

# God
# in
# Our
# Lives

# God, You Done Good!

AN ANCIENT BELIEF HOLDS that in the hereafter every person will have to give an account justifying permissible pleasures from which he or she abstained. Perhaps we wince. Is this an invitation to hedonism, the personal pursuit of pleasure as the chief goal of life? By no means. This statement does not come from some Hedonist Handbook. It comes from the Talmud, the centuries-old wisdom of Jewish rabbinical writings.

But it sure sounds suspect to a lot of Christians, especially Protestants influenced by Puritanism or Catholics still affected by Jansenism—the belief that the body is evil. These "isms" look upon pleasure and bodily needs as incompatible with holiness. Throughout vast periods of Christian history there has been an impression that one of the best things that could happen to us humans would be that we would be divested of our bodies. Being human was looked upon as risky. "Deny the flesh," was the admonition often given by solemn confessors. In medieval times, even spouses were considered guilty of sin if they enjoyed their lovemaking; it was supposed to be carried out only for procreation, not for personal enjoyment.

In interpreting this statement about permissible pleasures, the rabbis of old spoke holistically and voiced some wonderfully positive teachings. They did not see this as an invitation to hedonism, but to appreciation and worship. To them God was like a beneficent mother who has prepared a delicious meal for us, her children, by the creation of this physical world. What pleases her is when we accept and enjoy it. She likes to see us happy.

However, the rabbis made three important distinctions for enjoying the permissible pleasures of life. First, remember who gave them to us—God, our Creator, to whom we owe all we are and have. Enjoy them according to God's plan. Second, be genuinely thankful. Appreciate the gifts we have and let our hearts well up with gratitude to the One who loves us so much. Finally, don't forget to share these gifts with others. Be generous. Care for the poor and those in need. Don't hoard God's gifts.

How refreshing is this invitation and interpretation! Too often and for too long, many of us have maintained a subliminal attitude that God prefers to see us suffer and squirm. Tornadoes are acts of God, but beautiful days are from Mother Nature. We're almost afraid to let ourselves think that God invites us to experience the pleasures and joys of life—as though we almost can't trust ourselves to use them responsibly. Many a parent may fear, "If I told my kids anything like this rabbinical teaching they'd just think it's permission to run off and have sex." But this response misunderstands the teaching. The teaching does not encourage license or irresponsibility. The result of this misunderstanding is that our image of God suffers. God becomes chiefly a disciplinarian, a police officer, or a judge, rather than a loving parent, a mother who bakes her best pie just for us.

Studies show that when a human's image of God is that of a personal, loving Being who wants only good for us, morality and values are more developed than when God is imagined as fearsome. We tend to live up to love when we recognize that we are its recipients; we respond with much less dedication when we experience fear.

We live in a society increasingly unaware of God, where we came from, how valuable we are, and what love really means. We envy the appreciation of those early Jewish rabbis, or people like poet and storyteller Hondo Crouch, who said:

> Sad folks wake up and say, "Nuther day." I wake up and say, "There she is *again!* There it is!" Isn't it funny . . . all this pretty stuff doesn't happen unless I'm there.
>
> I get on my knees and pat the earth and say, "God, you done it again! God, you done good! Thank you, feller . . . friend!"

# The Virtue of Hope

THE DIPSTICK ON A CAR engine tells how much oil it has. When we allow the oil to become low, the engine is in danger of burning out. Without oil the engine's moving parts are not well lubricated, metal rubs against metal, friction and heat occur, and the engine seizes up. "Your oil is low," says the mechanic. "You'd better add another quart or so."

Life without hope is like an engine without oil. Life seizes up and burns out without hope. The events of life rub against one another, causing the heat of resentment and friction. What is hope? Hope is not merely a trivial "I wish . . ." or "I would like it if . . ." Hope is a conviction, an inner certainty about a positive future. Hope means believing in a bigger picture, and ultimately a God whose wonderful plan eventually happens.

The dipstick of our times tells us that the oil of hope is low. We feel the resulting heat in the higher level of anger and violence in society, disappointment with politicians and leaders, and gloom about the future. This attitude of pessimism varies in direct proportion to the frequency with which we follow world news. This is true not only because world news is depressing, but because we don't counterbalance world news with other factors. We lead political lives, not spiritual lives.

Having hope does not mean being a stagnant person, just waiting for the good times to come. Having hope means to cooperate actively with God in making them gradually come. An active hope causes involvement and gives meaning to life. Genuine hope is dynamic. It looks for the best in people, not for the worst. It discovers what can be done instead of complaining about what cannot. It looks at problems as opportunities, not as impenetrable walls. It pushes ahead when it would be easy to quit. It lights the proverbial candle instead of cursing the darkness. It believes instead of wimping out.

If our oil is low, how can we add a quart? How can we grow in hope? First, we must counterbalance the material with the spiritual, the world news with the Good News. Newspapers and television give only a part of the picture of reality. Parents, synagogues, churches, and schools are to give the other part. If solid religion and worship are not part of our lives, perhaps we ought to consider making them so.

Second, we can work at not running our motor so much. Slow down. Serious reading, thinking, discussion, silence are all imperative to whole, healthy persons. If television is our chief companion, no wonder we feel depressed. I see hope in the numbers of people in bookstores and taking walks. Small chapels and quiet places are becoming more sought after. We must look inside, not just outside, ourselves.

Third, we can develop loving relationships. An amazing interconnection between genuine loving and hoping. Love opens horizons, reveals another world, knows no end. Love instills a hope that looks forward from wherever we are, and reminds us of what can be.

The following verse was found on the wall of a German concentration camp. It had to have been written by a person with a hope that saw more than a pessimistic present.

I believe in the sun, even when it is not shining.
I believe in love, even when I feel it not.
I believe in God, even when he is silent.

# Thinking of Heaven

WE LIVE IN ONE OF THE most death-denying cultures that has ever existed. We abhor the thought of imperfection, suffering, and our own mortality. The illusion lingers in the back of our mind that we'll live here forever—if we just exercise, eat less fat, wear seat belts, and do for ourselves the endless "right things" we constantly hear about. Death, for most people, has nothing positive about it.

Yet perhaps a change is beginning. Movies, talk shows, and books about near-death experiences are beginning to insert a few positive aspects about dying amid our many fears. Some people, after being revived from the point of death, portray the process of dying as an experience of clarity and self-awareness, deep peacefulness, a sense of a loving God, and meeting relatives who have gone before. They say they are no longer as frightened about dying as they were before.

The vast majority of people believe in God and a continuation of life after this world. Although the concepts of hell and heaven are familiar in various religions, the truth seems to be that we do little thinking about heaven. We admit that heaven is supposed to be a wonderful place. But in our honest moments we have a sneaking suspicion that we just might find God and heaven rather boring. We wonder: "What will I do all day—just look at God?" "Will my dead pet be alive in heaven?" "What will I look like?" "Is there sex in heaven?" "Will there be any sports to watch or play?"

Let's think more expansively for a moment about heaven. Let's begin with ourselves and our human nature as we know it in this world (for we will always be humans whether we're here or in heaven). Philosophers have told us that all knowledge comes through the senses. What we experience comes from outside, through the channel of one or more of our five senses—touch, hearing, taste, sight, and smell. The knowledge and pulse of life come through all we experience via our senses. They are then integrated by our mind and incorporated into our person.

But who is to say that these five senses of ours are the only possible senses to the inner person? Suppose, for example, that we had fewer than five senses. Imagine that by nature we had only four senses, and sight was not one of them. Instead of seeing, we moved about and kept from bumping into things by sound waves we sent and received, like a bat. Lacking sight, we humans would be ignorant of all that sight brings. We would never know what is meant by the color red, or enjoy blue skies, paintings, or the beauty of the human form. We could not gaze upon mountains, stars, the spray of the surf, or a field full of flowers. If all humans had only four senses, and lacked sight, we wouldn't feel deprived because we would never even suspect the experience of sight existed.

Then suppose that when we died we came to the fullness of existence by receiving the sense of sight as well as thousands of other senses, or ways, of experiencing life, God, and one another. Would this be boredom? Far from it. These new senses connecting us with intense life and its Author would astound us and cause exhilaration. Life in heaven will be like turning new corners and finding surprises that thrill and fascinate us. Most especially, we'll love like we've never loved before, and we'll be loved unconditionally. Our relationships with God and others will be deep, personal, and intimate.

An inspired author of the Scriptures expresses the same preview of heaven when he writes, "What no eye has seen and no ear has heard, what the mind of man cannot visualise; all that God has prepared for those who love him" (1 Corinthians 2:9). We don't think of heaven enough as we journey here on earth. The anticipation of our destination can make the journey so much more tolerable.

# Faith: You Can't Wait 'Til You Need It

*FAITH* IS USUALLY CONSIDERED to be a spiritual term exclusively. But it also describes a very natural, human tendency. With the help of faith, we accept and believe what we can't see or prove. For example, if a friend phones and says he just bought a new car, we believe him even though we don't see the car. We believe a lot of things we don't actually see. We accept a lot that we can't prove. Faith and trust are constantly operative, even in mundane ways.

Used in a spiritual or supernatural way, faith means accepting and believing things that are beyond this world. The natural things of this world can be proven, and when something we first took on faith is subsequently proven, faith is no longer necessary. We stop having faith in our friend's words about his new car when we go to his house and see his new car. Then reason and physical proof take the place of faith.

But some things, extremely important things, are beyond this world. We can't go somewhere and physically prove these things to ourselves. We must either accept or reject them, for they go beyond the power of physical proof. I am speaking of the answers to questions like the following: Is there really a God? Do we still live after we die, or do we just evaporate at death? Does how we live, choose, and decide in this life affect a final, lasting life? Is there such a thing as a heaven or a hell that we choose by how we live now?

Each of us must answer these questions for ourselves. Just as no one can jog or exercise for us, no one can believe for us. Physical eyesight is a gift that enables us to see the world around us. Faith is a gift of spiritual eyesight, offered by God, that enables us to

17

see farther than physical sight or reason alone. It permits us to believe what we can't see, accept what we can't prove, and trust in a providential plan behind all the apparent irrationalities of life. One of the most commonly asked questions in life is "Why?" Why did my baby die? Why do we suffer? Why am I not satisfied despite all that I own? Why did I lose my job after all I've done for the company? Why, why, to a thousand questions. To many, a trusting faith is often the only valid answer. It is often more plausible than other clever or simplistic explanations.

However, a faith that helps us cope with such important questions of life does not happen quickly or come easily—unless we're the recipients of a miracle. Usually an adult faith, a mature faith, is one that has grown over the years and become deeply our own. Grace, reason, and much thought are important in developing an intense faith, but in the final analysis, faith is a leap into the unprovable. It usually occurs only after we have lived enough and suffered enough. It's premature to expect it of children and adolescents, or people who are very controlled, self-sufficient, or whose god is their own intellect.

The time to be growing and increasing our own faith is now, not when a tragedy strikes or we learn that we have a short time to live. We can't just expect faith to appear when it is needed. Sometimes our sufferings throughout life, or at its end, are compounded by not having the inner support of faith.

But how do we develop a healthy and solid faith? Above all, we need to open our hearts and unclutter our lives to make room for the graces and gifts God wants to give us. We need to ponder the Scriptures frequently and deeply, read solid spiritual books, have discussions with levelheaded, faith-filled people who leave us free but offer their insights. We need to pray, to talk with God even if we wonder whether God is really there. Attending regular worship services is also very helpful. Amid all the words, hymns, preaching, and music at a church worship, the grace of God moves. It accomplishes more than the sum of all the human aspects of the service, and slowly enlightens us. God has surprising ways of getting through to us and convincing us of God's presence, love, and trustworthiness. Then faith seems the only valid answer to the mystery of life.

# The Providence of God

THE WORD *PROVIDENCE* is probably not in our everyday vocabulary. It comes from two Latin words: *pro* (for) and *videre* (to see). It carries the connotation of someone "looking out for" someone else. Theologically, various religions understand the concept with different shades of meaning, but in general, providence means that God looks out for each of us. Not only does it matter to God how our life is going, but in some mysterious way God is also involved, working in our lives. This involvement is subtle and leaves us completely free to make our own choices. Nevertheless, God is there working for our good. From this perspective, a coincidence is a minor miracle in which God wishes to remain anonymous. If we look closely, our lives have a lot of coincidences. Usually we notice them only in hindsight.

Most of us feel we're dealing with life all alone. And we struggle to understand why various incidents take place in our lives. Events can seem so random, even chaotic, and their logic escapes us.

One explanation for the haphazard events of our lives, according to existential nihilists, is that there is no God behind them, no rhyme or reason to things. Everything is basically absurd. Life "is a tale / Told by an idiot, full of sound and fury, / Signifying nothing," says Shakespeare's Macbeth. The other possible explanation is that life is a story with the greatest of all meanings, and a mysterious, awesome mind, heart, and plan lie behind it. There is a bigger picture. We can't step back and see this big picture yet because we're still *in* the picture. Although our desire is to know reasons, perceive causes, understand the logic, and be in control of it all, our full knowing comes only in time—indeed, only after time.

There is great wisdom in the story of an old Chinese man who was very poor. One day the only horse he had ran off and disappeared into the hills. Seeing his "bad luck," friends came to sympathize with him. But the old man just smiled and said, "Who knows what's good, what's bad?"

The next day the farmer's horse returned home leading ten other wild horses. He and his son quickly corralled them. When the villagers saw this they hurried over to congratulate the farmer on his "good luck," for all these horses made him a wealthy man. But the wise farmer once again smiled and said to them, "Who knows what's good, what's bad?"

Some days later, while trying to train one of the new horses, the farmer's son fell and broke his leg. Knowing how much the farmer depended on his son, the old man's neighbors came to commiserate with him when they heard the bad news. But the old man calmly smiled and said once again, "Who knows what's good, what's bad?"

Two days later a marauding group of bandits came riding through and forcefully conscripted all the young men in the village to go with them to fight a battle. But they did not take the old man's son because his broken leg made him useless to them. When the bandits left, back came his neighbors, who joyfully congratulated him that his son was spared and he still had him. Once again the farmer wryly smiled and said, "Who knows what's good, what's bad?"

Life is often ambiguous and complex. We try to live morally, understand as much as we can, and make responsible choices, but in truth we know we do not always see the bigger picture or understand the wider view. We don't always grasp the reasons for the randomness, the tragedies, or even the unexpected joys of life. We don't always know what's good, what's bad.

To those who do not believe in a provident God, no explanation is possible. To those who do, no explanation is necessary.

# How Small We Are, How Little We Know

WE DON'T ALWAYS REALIZE when momentous events are happening. A spectacular scientific event has slowly unfolded over recent years. If proven true, it will be as important as when we realized that the sun doesn't revolve around the Earth. Commenting on this event's importance, President Clinton said, "It speaks of the possibility of life. If this discovery is confirmed, it will surely be one of the most stunning insights into our universe that science has ever uncovered."

What's been happening? In 1984, a team of scientists in Antarctica found a meteorite the size of a potato. In the years since, NASA researchers have determined that the meteorite came to Earth from Mars thirteen thousand years ago, after being sent into orbit when an asteroid collided with Mars sixteen million years before that. Geochemist Dr. David McKay announced that within the rock there appeared to be chemical and fossil remains of microscopic organisms that lived on Mars 3.6 billion years ago. If this proves to be true, it will be the first time there has been evidence of living organisms anywhere in the universe besides Earth.

Commenting on this amazing discovery, Bill Broadway, a columnist for the *Washington Post,* wrote, "Proof of life on other planets, whether microscopic and dumb or human-size and intelligent, would only confirm the expansive nature of God taught in every major religion." It's understandable, then, that this discovery makes our mind and imagination wonder about our universe, our own human nature, and other possible universes and natures out there in the endlessness of space.

Some people see the possibility of other life, lesser or greater than our own, as a blow to our pride. We who think we know everything and like to see ourselves as unique, powerful, and in control might have to change our perspective. What if, in this or other universes, there exist vastly different and superior intelligent beings? What if this God, who some of us try so desperately to ignore or elude, actually exists and is magnificently greater and more abundantly creative than we ever thought?

One of our chief tendencies in thinking about God is to anthropomorphize—to think that God is similar to us, possessing our human limitations and restrictions. We think that divinity is defined by humanity. How conceited! God is utterly beyond our mind, even our imagination. The very fact that we are stunned by possible scientific proof that life in other forms exists on another planet is evidence of how we limit God. Do we actually imagine that we are the extent of God's creative power? Do we not flatter ourselves by thinking that this universe, and we alone, burst forth from the dazzling mind of this brilliant, eternal Being?

God created us not because of loneliness, boredom, or the need for an audience. God is complete, satisfied, ecstatically and eternally happy. God creates out of goodness. A principle in scholastic philosophy puts it well: *bonum est diffusivum sui,* or "good is diffusive of itself." If we find something especially good, delicious, or beautiful, we feel compelled to share that goodness with others, and say: "Hey, taste this, you'll love it!" or, "Look at that, isn't it beautiful?" God, thrilling to the goodness of existence, creates out of a loving desire to share it with other rational beings. God creates each of us, introduces us to life, and says, "Come alive! It can really be terrific!" Do we think we are the only rational beings to whom God says this?

In the past, science has sometimes been seen as the enemy of religion, the opponent of God. Lately, as we open our mind and scientists open theirs, science affirms God and hints at a magnificent divine intellect, power, and plan. Eventually, all scientific findings will continue to lead us to wonder and marvel at the existence and nature of a God we have underestimated. We will discover that God is more unlike what we think than like what we think. God is ultimate Mystery.

If that rock from Mars says what it seems to say, it will not only have great scientific significance, but spiritual significance as well. It will intensify our inner searching and the spiritual revival that is occurring as we enter the twenty-first century. God has a way of getting us to pay attention when we most need to.

# Our
# Morality
# Is
# Really
# an
# Answer

MANY YEARS AGO, WHEN I was a young man, a beautiful young woman told me that she loved me. She was the first who ever did so with such genuine words and feelings. I'll never forget that moment; none of us forgets that first love. Although this event is repeated time and again by other men and women, our own time is our special treasure.

Such times mean so much to us because they are times of emotional self-revelation. The young woman revealed to me what was deep within her heart. On one hand, she was risking herself, offering her heart to me. On the other hand, her self-revelation called for a response from me, perhaps reciprocity or rejection. Such deeply personal revelations ask for an answer: Do you love me, too?

Jewish, Catholic, Protestant, we all believe there is a God who chose to be revealed to us. God is especially revealed in the sacred Scriptures, but also within our consciences and the events of life. One of the most remarkable self-revelations made to us humans is that God loves us, each of us, all of us. And the same dynamic is operative as when that young lady stood before me years ago and told me she loved me. Just as she offered her heart, so does God. And God's self-revelation awaits our response to the same unspoken question: Do you love me, too? In the language of religion, our response is called our "morality."

Moral theology attempts to discern the implications of God's existence and love for us. Or, to put it another way, moral theology asks, "How should I behave and live in view of the fact that God exists and loves me? If I love in return, how do I express that reciprocal love in all areas of my life? Should I do

23

everything I feel like doing or, if I love God, are there some things I should choose to do or not do because of that love?"

One of the "isms" around today is secular humanism. From the perspective of secular humanism, when we make decisions, there is no one to take into account other than ourselves and our world—not a Divine Being who made me, loves me, and awaits my response. The only motivation and measure of my behavior is me, my needs and desires in this world.

Many of us seem to make choices today as if we are the only ones to be considered in our decision making. We seem to leave a loving God totally out of the picture of our lives. Analogously, it's as if, on the special day when that beautiful girl told me she loved me, I had behaved as if I were the only one there, ignoring the fact that someone was offering her heart and awaiting a response. At such a time, however, we must have a morality, we must respond. The answer may be "Yes," "No," or "I don't know," but we must respond.

Our morality is so important because it is our response to God's offer of love. It is often difficult to know exactly what comprises a loving response to God, for life is often complex. Yet on other occasions it is not so difficult, for we know that God has asked us to be fair, compassionate, and loving to one another. So if we truly love God, we include God in our decision making and try very hard to find the fair, honest, and caring thing to do in situations we face. Then we honestly choose to carry it out. In so doing, we're each saying to this Eternal Beauty, "I love you, too."

# Richard the Atheist

"I'M RICHARD THE ATHEIST" is how he introduces himself. He often eats at a small restaurant in the eastern part of the city. In this setting he is likely to be seated at a counter shoulder-to-shoulder with people he's never met before. He's a friendly man, laughs readily, and engages people in conversation. But he watches for opportunities to guide the conversation to the topic of religion. Once there, he can express himself on the foibles of organized religion and the ridiculousness of believing in God. He does so jovially, but with a certain belittling humor that makes some people feel put-upon or embarrassed.

What amazes me is his obsession with talking about the God he says doesn't exist. He's been talking about God for years. I often wonder, "Why spend that much time, thought, and effort talking about someone who allegedly isn't there?" You and I don't believe in the Tooth Fairy, so we never think of her or talk about her. If we hear parents suggest that their small child put an extracted tooth under the pillow hoping for a surprise from the Tooth Fairy, we don't feel it necessary to prove that she's a figment of the child's imagination. Nor do we steer people's conversations to the topic in order to belittle the Tooth Fairy. If we did, psychologists might have a field day analyzing whether our preoccupation implies that we think she actually exists.

Which all makes me think that Richard the Atheist isn't an atheist at all; he's an agnostic. An agnostic is in the middle-ground position between a "theist" (a person who believes there is a God) and an "atheist" (who believes there is no God). An agnostic isn't prepared to commit one way or the other. He or she just "doesn't know" (the meaning of the word *agnostic* is "not to know"). It has been said that the prayer of an agnostic would go something like, "O God, if there is a God, save my soul, if I have a soul."

Should I step forward some day and try to prove to Richard that there is a God? That's impossible. Although Thomas Aquinas offered his "Five Proofs for the Existence of God" centuries ago, one person cannot prove to another that there is or isn't a God. That is a matter of faith. Faith and love are similar. More than just emotions, faith and love are essentially acts of the will. A person chooses to believe, a person chooses to love. I cannot make people believe in a God any more than I can make them love someone passionately. I can help predispose them to belief in God. Reason and logic can go a long way—but eventually the person who believes or loves has to leap, or not leap. Atheists turn back from the leap, theists jump into invisible arms they are convinced are there, and agnostics stand on the brink, unsure whether to leap.

What will become of Richard? Were I to guess, I'd say there will be a day when he'll leap into the arms of the God he now questions. Why do I think that? Because Richard seems like an honest man, very human, with a certain love in his heart for other people. And whenever that is true, a person has already made a first acquaintance with God, whether she or he knows it or not. For, as one of the Scripture writers so aptly puts it, "Everyone who loves is born of God and knows God. Whoever does not love does not know God, for God is love" (1 John 4:7–8).

# The Dance of Our Spiritual Lives

"WHAT'S BEST FOR ME?" we may wonder. "Should I get another job?" "Should I major in business or engineering?" "Should I stay in this marriage or get out?" "Should I have the operation or wait?" "Should I tell him or not?" Decisions always need to be made, some great, some small. We know that we are affecting our lives and our happiness by what we decide, so we struggle with decisions.

As we struggle, whom do we take into account? Ourselves, of course. We want to be happy, healthy, prosperous, loved—so we try to choose what will accomplish that. Besides ourselves, we often take other people into account, such as our parents, spouse, children, and close friends. Our lives touch others, so we try to make good decisions that consider them as well.

Yet, there's someone else to also take into account. A Carthusian monk put it this way: "The spiritual life is like a dance with a partner who has a fertile imagination and who leads. We must be alert, responsive to the slightest indication of his intention, supple, ready to adapt to the movements with which he woos us." If we believe in God, and realize that God is even more concerned with our happiness than we are, then life, with all its struggles and decisions, is a spiritual life. And it is truly like a dance in which we are being subtly led around the floor. We can be klutzy and resistant, breaking the flow of the dance, or we can sense the gentle directions of the One who leads, and follow as best we can. It takes two to dance well to the rhythm of life.

27

This is what our spiritual life is, paying closer and closer attention to the soft nudgings of God. Mention "spiritual life," however, and we usually think of something separate from the ordinary decisions of life. We think that spiritual life happens only in a church or a temple, or when we're praying. We don't realize that the spiritual part of our person is involved in everything we do and choose. It's down in the core, or center, of our person where God tries to dance with us. Spirituality has to do with guiding us into meaning, purpose, happiness, and real joy—it is hardly dull or unimportant. Carl Jung said that unless we deal well with the spiritual area of life, we will not be as happy as we could be.

To follow the lead of God requires close attention, for God's way may be different than the way we want to go. Sometimes God's dance steps are hard to learn. God's lead may indicate to one person to keep working at a marriage he or she wants to leave, and to another person to leave a marriage because a great mistake was made and a destructive, unhealthy relationship now exists. God's lead may suggest to one person that he is paying too much attention to the material, human aspects of life, and to another that she is not paying enough attention to the same aspects. In our spirituality, we try to sense the touch of God on our person, and follow it.

We find it difficult to become attuned to our Divine Partner because we forget that God is there, or we like to control the dance ourselves, or we keep so busy we don't know how to sense the intimate touch that is leading. That's too bad. The dance of life could be the most exciting one we've ever attended.

# Does Our Prayer Matter?

FOR MANY WEEKS THAT seemed too long, my brother, sisters, and I assisted our mother as she suffered from terminal cervical cancer. She was eighty-eight years old, had lived a long, good life, and had done her level best in raising her children virtually by herself. Needless to say, especially to those who have endured the same situation, it is hard to watch a parent draw toward death, especially when pain is involved. No matter how many years we have had their presence, it is never the right time to say good-bye.

In this situation, we prayed. Just like many other people, we prayed for health and healing or for a peaceful death. Before an operation or a job interview, or for a thousand and one other needs, people pray. In disasters such as hurricanes, earthquakes, plane crashes, or terrorist bombings, many people readily admit they pray.

Others, however, consider praying to be a sort of primitive religiosity. They believe that God is, in the last analysis, an inexorable fate from whom we can't ask anything. These people become "primitive" only when their backs are to the wall; or, if they can't pray even then, they become stoic, fatalistic, or give way to despair as existential nihilists.

All religions have prayers of petition that ask something of God. When we truly pray, it is not the demonstration of a childish or primitive religiosity but an expression of a basic, essential relationship—that we are creatures who have come from and exist according to the will of a Creator. The prayer of petition from creature to Creator acknowledges that relationship and our total dependence. It comes from a person humbly aware that she or he is not self-sufficient.

But does it matter that we pray? Theologians make all kinds of distinctions about God's changelessness and absolute freedom, the permanence of the will of God, and so on. They tell us not to expect the natural laws that God has put in place in the universe to be changed just because we ask. We are reminded of the harder task of adjusting our will to God's, not God's to ours. They tell us of a bigger picture that God sees that includes not only joys, pleasures, and happiness but also suffering, loss, illness, and death. They remind us that God's ways are above our ways and that God even brings greater good out of apparent defeat. And all that is true. Yet there are times when we must set all that aside and just pray.

Karl Rahner, one of the greatest Catholic theologians of the twentieth century, observed that God, the Creator of all, "has become very approachable and easily moved." He continues:

> There is a prayer of petition which speaks to God and is not a mere exorcism of one's own heart, but boldly and explicitly ventures to ask him for bread, peace, restraint of his enemies, health, the spread of his kingdom on earth, and a host of such earthly and highly problematic things.
>
> That such a prayer combines a great measure of "self-will" (for one presents to him one's *own* desires) with a supreme degree of submissiveness (for one *prays* to him whom one cannot compel, persuade, or charm, but only beg), that here there is a mingling and an incomprehensible fusion of the greatest boldness with the deepest humility . . . this makes the prayer of petition in one respect not the lowest but the highest, the most divinely human form of prayer.

So, we humans pray. We pray buoyed by our faith, our hope, our necessities, our trust that whatever the answer, it will be the best answer. Perhaps Tennyson put it most succinctly: "More things are wrought by prayer / Than this world dreams of."

# How Grown-up Is Our Religion?

"IN PROBABLY NO REGION of personality do we find so many residues of childhood as in the religious attitudes of adults." So wrote Gordon W. Allport of Harvard University in his classic study *The Individual and His Religion.* It is a key observation in his study of the religious development of the mature personality.

The point of Allport's statement is not to diminish religion or religious people, but to encourage religious growth and maturity. He recognizes the importance of the spiritual dimension of life and the need for it to grow.

His observation is sobering. He's saying that we adults tend to remain the most childish in the ways we think of God and consider our religion. We grow more mature in so many other areas of life—in our understanding of mathematics, science, business, investment skills, computers, and so on—but all the while we hang on to childish attitudes in understanding the ways of God. Theology, the study of God, for centuries was known as the "Queen of the Sciences." Why? Because God is ultimate Mystery and the study of God was considered the deepest exploration the human mind could make. But today the average person is not interested in the pursuit of this mystery. We find it boring, and it has no apparent practical or financial purpose. As a result, for the rest of our adult lives our childhood images and understandings ("residues," in Allport's term) of religion define our religious perspectives in the midst of the complexities of adult life.

But mature religious development does have a great practical impact on the way we deal with the issues of life. Without mature spiritual insights, we are left ill equipped to face questions about life, death, suffering, contemporary moral problems, and crucial issues of a spiritual nature. Many people, in the face of death or serious problems, ask questions based on lingering childhood attitudes about religion, and often express resentment rather than faith or insight. "Why is God doing this to me?" one might ask, as though God likes to see us suffer. We settle moral struggles with simplistic solutions: "This is a free country, so we can do what we want"; "Traditional values are out-of-date"; "Suffering has no purpose—do anything to avoid it." Theologically, childhood attitudes lead us to think in terms of black and white, making complex concepts overly simple.

In his book, Allport describes some attributes of more mature, adult religious attitudes. A mature religion is well differentiated—it is reflective and critical, recognizing the difference between essentials and less important accidentals. It grows over time and becomes more and more free of the egocentric concerns of childhood, when religion was just a way to get what we want.

Another attribute, says Allport, is that the religion of maturity is dynamic. That means that it truly affects and directs our whole life, motives, and behavior—we walk what we talk. At the same time, it is balanced, not fanatical or compulsive, and has a realistic view of life and humanness.

A third attribute that Allport proposes is that mature religion is also heuristic, or open. Our religious convictions are held in a tentative way until, through deeper study, reflection, and prayer, they intensify and grow more valid. They are like a working hypothesis that helps us find better and truer answers to the problems of life as we live it. This necessitates that we eventually lay aside some childish concepts in order to expand our smaller, human thoughts into grander, more divine ones. Adults who are growing more mature in their religion keep realizing that the God they thought they knew was far too small.

"The religion of maturity makes the affirmation 'God is,' but only the religion of immaturity will insist, 'God is precisely what I say He is,'" writes Allport. The twenty-first century is here. May it be an era when we set aside childish diffidence and peer maturely into that mystery we grasp so little—the God who made us.

# Hell, No! Hell, Yes!

WHAT ABOUT HELL? IN THIS enlightened time of history, does the concept of hell still have a place in religious belief?

Hell has a varied history. At times it is depicted as populated by fallen angels and humans, or characterized by red men with long tails, horns, and pitchforks; it has been described in literature by Dante and in scriptural texts as a place of torment, fire, and pain; it is portrayed as a place of finality from which no one leaves.

Because many of us end our religious education in childhood, these kinds of images remain in the adult mind. Such childhood images convey a storybook quality that many adults only half believe. Most don't know what to do with the concept of hell, especially when they try to balance it with a loving God. "I don't see how a loving God could send someone to hell forever," is a common objection. Hell remains vague and considered by some as only a scare tactic to prompt good living.

In fact, the concept of being "sent" to hell is erroneous. It implies that we really want God but God does not want us, and sends us away. This understanding compares God to a human judge who sends us to jail as we plead that we don't want to go. But we have been given many gifts, including the gift of genuine freedom, and we are free to choose God or not choose God in the decisions we make in our lives. Being free, we cannot be forced to choose God, and over a lifetime we freely choose, and we get what we choose. Hell, then, has to do with freedom. If life continues after this world, and if human beings are truly free, then hell is as much a possibility as heaven.

Theologians speak of what is called our "fundamental option." This means that over a lifetime we gradually develop a basic option or pattern of choosing: I opt for what I want to do, or what God wants me to do. God wants honesty, but I can choose to lie; God wants respect for another's property, but I can choose to steal it; God wants me to love and be faithful to my spouse, but I can choose to be unfaithful. I am constantly choosing God's way or my way. I'm free to choose either way.

If I made a graph of the days and years of my life, like a graph of the stock market, I would see two things. First, I would see that there are a lot of little ups and downs. The days my line goes down are when I selfishly choose my way even if it means going against what God wants. The days my line goes up are when I choose God's way, sometimes even at great inconvenience or sacrifice. There are a lot of jagged ups and downs in all our lives.

The second thing I'd notice on the graph of my life is that the overall trend of my life choices is gradually going up or down over the years. The downward trend means that God means less and less to me as I make my choices. I am basically opting for myself, not others, not God. That self-chosen downward line is heading toward a condition called hell, a condition of being in which God is absent. Through our essential gift of freedom, we get what we have chosen. Yet we burn with regret and emptiness. The regret comes from realizing that what I have chosen, myself only, is not enough for me. I missed everything and everyone, especially God. And to realize that is hell!

# The
# God
# I
# Don't
# Believe
# In

THE GOD I DO NOT BELIEVE in is the God of our own making, the God that is fabricated from ignorance, pathology, or small human minds. I can understand why some people find it hard to believe in God or to join organized religion. The image of God they see presented to them by other people is often a God I could not believe in either. It's often a God who is severe and capricious rather than loving, a God who is characterized by rules and legalistic attitudes rather than exquisite sensitivity and justice. Some of the traits we foist on God are those that good humans would never envision in themselves.

I don't believe in a God who is insensitive to our pain. Horrendous things occur in the lives of many humans—premature death, accidents, betrayal by friends, painful illnesses and losses, and so on. Friends of mine lost their infant son to a tragic disease. Well-meaning acquaintances said, "I guess God just wanted another angel in heaven." Unfortunately, that logic paints an awful picture. It depicts an insensitive and cruel God who took away their son and purposely caused them great pain to satisfy some alleged divine need. I cannot believe that God likes to see us suffer, just as I cannot believe that good parents like to see their children suffer. Suffering is part of life in this world, some caused by the unfinished nature of this world, some by the ignorance and malice of others, some by our own actions. I believe in a God who hurts when we hurt, who is with us in the midst of our pain, and who is powerful enough to bring good for us out of our suffering.

I don't believe in a God who is my puppet. When I was younger and very spiritually naive, I imagined that what I thought was best was always best. If I prayed and asked for something, God would give it to me. If I lived well, God would be indebted to me. How could I be denied if I was a good boy for God? I foolishly thought that God could be bargained with, manipulated, cajoled, or fooled. God was my servant, my puppet.

Now that I am older I perceive how little I know of the mysterious, awesome nature of God. Although I'm often lost in trying to figure out God's mysterious ways, I depend on God. I trust in the farseeing love God has for me, for you, for us all. I still pray and ask for things. I struggle with that old tendency to become angry when what I pray for doesn't happen. I understand, however, that the result of much of my praying is not just to get what I want, but to be made stronger in the face of my problems. And I continue to believe and be thankful even when I don't get what I want.

I don't believe in a God who is less than I am. There is this suspicion in the back of our mind that we are somehow more wise, more loving, more intelligent than God. We think, "If I were God for a day I'd do things a lot better." That's the thinking of someone whose faith overlooks God's incomprehensible nature. The people of the early biblical days thought that God was so great and mysterious that if they ever saw God they would die. Today we think that if we ever saw God we would be bored. God is infinitely more than anything we are. Any degree of love, wisdom, knowledge, or insight we possess is only a hint of God's.

The God I can believe in—and really *want* to believe in—is the One whose presence is already felt by anything that is true, good, and beautiful, and by the hungers we have in our hearts that go unsatisfied by this world.

# The Messiness of It All

"IN THE BEGINNING," things were dark, turbulent, and chaotic. That's how the Book of Genesis depicts the scene in which God first drew near to create this world. It was certainly not a pretty picture. God began by bringing order and beauty to the messiness: "Let there be light!" "Let there be animals, flowers, sun, moon, and stars!" "Let there be humans in my image and likeness!"

Our illusions about happiness lead us to think it will come to us easily and only from sweet, pleasant, orderly situations. We still think we will get married and live happily ever after, and that wealth brings happiness.

These illusions also affect Christians in the way they look at Christmas. Christians believe that God came close to Earth once again on that first Christmas in the person of Jesus Christ. They celebrate it by constructing pretty crib scenes of Mary, Joseph, and Jesus. Christians depict wide-eyed shepherds and little lambs in a stable with sparkles in the straw, and play sentimental songs in the background. Christians make the coming of God into this world seem pretty, picturesque, and tranquil. That's all well and good. Are we to conclude, however, that whenever God comes into our life it will be a similarly romantic event? Or does the coming of God more usually occur in the dark, turbulent, chaotic times that beset us?

The birth of Jesus Christ was an awesome event, more wonderful than we can imagine. We try to commemorate it with extraordinary creativity and beauty. Yet a brief reflection on the reality of that first Christmas indicates that it was as ordinary, complex, and messy as our lives are now. There was the anxiety of a man, Joseph, worried about his fiancée's unexplained pregnancy and what to do about it. There was a woman, Mary, living an ordinary life and confused by the sudden string of events that included her pregnancy and marriage. There was a recent law forcing them to travel in the last stage of her pregnancy, and with travel came the fear of roadside robbers. There was no place to stay, a borrowed stable for a birthplace, the smell of manure, and efforts to keep the baby warm, find food, and get medical attention if needed. There was a certain messiness to it all—a combination of inconvenience, stress, worry, and confusion.

We need to remember this about the coming of God into our own lives. We expect the coming of God to be pretty and clean. It is supposed to happen in a chapel with the organ playing and a choir singing. We believe that it will be under reasonable circumstances, according to our expectations, and with a certain softness and beauty.

In my years as a clergyman, I have had the privilege of being closely associated with many people at key moments in their lives. As they open their lives and hearts to me, I learn more and more about how God usually comes to be known. It's often in those dark, turbulent, chaotic times—just like at the beginning of the world or at Bethlehem. It's in the messiness of life. God comes close to the woman whose husband has suddenly left her for another woman; to a couple with a sick infant; to a man trying to kick drugs; to a teenager struggling with depression; to a woman with a questionable mammogram; to parents worrying about their son or daughter; to a man who has lost his job. These are the messy times of life we call problems. They keep our lives from being as pretty and nice as we would like.

The God I know doesn't send us trouble. Trouble finds us, the way it found Jesus, Mary, and Joseph in the course of living out their lives. But God often uses those times to reach us and be born within us. Why must things be so messy? It has to do with learning to be human. It has to do with our ego needing to be broken open enough to let others in, even God. It has to do with learning how to love, trust, and believe.

May God come to be known in the midst of our lives. And just as "in the beginning," may God bring forth beauty from the messiness that is inevitably there.

# Saint?
# Holy?
# Who,
# Me?

WHAT DOES IT MEAN TO BE a saint? One answer might be, "To be outstanding in holiness." The logical next question is, "What does it mean to be holy?" That's where it starts going downhill. Concepts like saint and holiness seem archaic, even undesirable, to most people today. Who thinks in terms of being holy or saintly? We think more in terms of being sexy, rich, or famous. In fact, most of us enjoy having people think we're a little *un*saintly, *un*holy. Aren't all the good things of human life incompatible with holiness?

Not necessarily. Maybe our image of holiness is askew. Too many of us equate holiness with being boring and somber. Too many of us have images of pietistic people like those once used by French novelist Julien Green: ". . . A few bigots who smell of solid piety from ten feet away. A few thin and lofty-looking women, with the disagreeable air appropriate to those certain of their own virtue." If those are holy people, who wants to be one?

When I think of holiness and saintliness I think more in terms of what Saint Irenaeus said nineteen centuries ago: "The Glory of God is a human being who is fully alive!" God didn't make us human and then say, "Don't be human!" Becoming a saint, being holy, means becoming more and more human in the best possible sense. If Irenaeus is right, God wants us to be ourselves, our *best* selves. God delights in seeing us grow, for that is what God wanted at our creation. Before we diminished the word *holy,* it meant "whole" and "well balanced." We can reclaim that meaning.

We humans are very deep and complex. We have so many parts to our personalities. We so easily get off balance or go to extremes. We concentrate on the material and ignore the spiritual; we love sexuality but forget about responsible relationships; we love getting and possessing things, and too easily forget about giving and being. Becoming whole doesn't mean getting rid of our humanness, but putting all these aspects of humanness together.

It's extremely difficult to get ourselves in balance—so much so that we need a long time and the help of God. But as we achieve this balance, we begin to feel serene and joyful. We experience the fulfilling awareness that we're being just what we were made to be. We become more alive, not less alive. We become enthusiastic, not bored. Irenaeus thought that's just what God wants. God wants roses to grow and bloom, birds to stretch wings and fly; God wants us to become whole humans in all the parts of our person, not to be lopsided or self-centered.

We become saints and achieve wholeness usually without even realizing it. As we make our daily efforts to open ourselves to God, work through our pains and problems, relate well with our family and friends, we grow more whole. I like to think of the nitty-gritty events of life as the "stuff of holiness." Many times I am privileged to listen to people pour out their heart about their problems. I listen as they describe all that they are doing to cope and put their lives together. Most of the time, all I can do for them is listen, but as I listen I am humbled by the awareness that I am in the presence of a fellow human becoming a saint. I am inspired by them to do likewise.

# Awareness: If I Should Wake Before I Die

SOMEONE ASKED ME recently, "What do you think is the most common human weakness?" I answered, "A lack of awareness." We miss so much. We tend to think superficially, live busily, and settle for the shallows. We don't really know ourselves or the life we possess. We spend too much time being angry, feeling sorry for ourselves, or running in circles. We are unaware of the depth and texture of life. Opportunities pass by ungrasped and deeper appreciations of ourselves and others are never reached.

I like the way the late Fr. Anthony de Mello, a Jesuit spiritual writer, spoke of our need for awareness. He equated becoming more aware with becoming more spiritual. He said:

> Spirituality means waking up. Most people, even though they don't know it, are asleep. They're born asleep, they live asleep, they marry in their sleep, they breed children in their sleep, they die in their sleep without ever waking up. They never understand the loveliness and beauty of this thing that we call human existence.

Psychologists claim much the same thing. They just use different terminology, saying we live with too many "illusions," "practice denial," or "engage in projections." It's another way of saying that we don't see things as they are, that we don't deal with reality.

Why would becoming more aware be considered being more spiritual? Because spirituality is the opposite of physicality, which means living just on the surface of the physical world, as insects and animals do. Spirituality is that dimension of life that goes

41

beyond the material. It goes further than the objects and the horizon we see with our natural eyes. When we become aware, we see with inner eyes. We "see" things like meaning, motivation, and mystery. We "see" what our life is all about. We more easily tolerate the imperfections and appreciate the uniqueness of the people we love, and we grasp how fortunate we are that they love us, making us the choice of their heart. Remember the story of the person who wept as he held his dying friend in his arms? He sobbed, "You can't die, I never told you how much I love you!" We can be so asleep that we forget to say or do the things we most need to. Awareness, spirituality, bids us to wake up to life and love, and to act on what is really true.

A few people become acutely awake and aware. They are called mystics. Mystics are people who have developed the ability to wake up to the things of life that really matter. They are in close touch with all dimensions of their human nature. They are so awake that they look at life realistically *and* enthusiastically. Many of the things we worry about excessively don't matter much to them; and many things we consider insignificant are, to them, priceless.

Mystics are people who need periods of solitude and silence in their lives. In solitude and silence they expand their soul and become more in touch with themselves. They're not fake people. They don't play games. They can have a certain calmness even in the midst of troubles. Their troubles and sufferings hurt and lead them to weep, but their perspective and wisdom offer understanding. Mystics don't seem to be exactly on the same wavelength as the masses of people, so they are considered a little different. Waking up has its price, even though it's immensely fulfilling.

We are all called to be mystics, in a sense. We don't have to live in a monastery or a hermitage. We may have children to raise or a demanding job. Yet somewhere in it all we need to find opportunities for silence and honesty, for reading solid books, for discussing life reflectively with others. Most of all we need to begin that inward journey that winds down into the core of our person. Sometimes we need a psychologist, spiritual counselor, or already-awake friend to assist us. At other times, we can travel alone and slowly waken ourselves. At first, waking up tends to frighten us, for reality can be harsh before it is wonderful. But as we continue awakening we'll notice that we have the tendency to do something else—smile and be glad of where we are.

# Getting Older, Getting Younger

Is it possible to grow older and younger at the same time? Certainly. It's possible to experience contrary situations. For example, our bank account can be growing, making us richer by the day, yet we can feel threatened that we don't have enough; we can study more and remember less, or socialize a lot and still feel lonely. It's the same with growing older and younger.

The English language sometimes hampers our understanding. We have only one word—*life*—with which to name our very existence. The Greek language has two words for life, *bios* and *zoe*. *Bios* means the natural or biological life we have as living organisms. It is the same life we have in common with other organisms such as plants, worms, dogs, and polar bears. *Bios* is limited and eventually perishes. *Zoe,* on the other hand, refers to an eternal element of life that never perishes, a share in the principle of life itself. When we grow in our soul, we grow in *zoe,* we become more fully alive and imperishable—in a sense, we become younger. Psychologists such as Jung and Kunkel believed that in the process called individuation a person gradually comes to partake of this inner aliveness. Many religions also believe that by becoming truly ourselves and genuinely loving, a divine principle of life grows in us and we come to possess a new kind of life essentially different from *bios*. Jung spoke of those who do not develop in this way as the living dead.

Almost all our time and energy is spent thinking about the *bios* kind of life. Growing old is looked at as a tragedy, midlife as a crisis, and death as the end of everything. We watch *bios*-life decline with trepidation. We fail to realize that at the same time as *bios* declines, *zoe* can be growing. They are meant to head in different directions. As one ebbs, the other is supposed to grow.

Growing old means moving *away* from the beginning of *bios*-life; growing young means moving *toward* the principle of *zoe*-life. A ten-year-old is older than a five-year-old because she or he has moved farther away from the beginning of *bios*-life. But a fifty-year-old person can be younger in her or his soul than a thirty-year-old if she or he has moved farther in the direction of the divine principle of *zoe*-life in her or his spiritual and psychological development. Wisdom, enjoyment, and true spiritual living can increase as the biological life declines. Fulfilled, serene, loving older persons are a joy to behold. We instinctively admire them.

Many people today are fascinated with the idea of near-death experiences. In books on the subject, people claim that dramatic events happened to them when they were at the point of death. Although they don't put it in exactly these words, as they reached the dreaded end of the *bios* kind of life, instead of fear they experienced great peace, fullness, and the fulfillment of their religious faith and convictions. They felt young, free, and exuberant again, as though they were close to the Source of life (the *zoe* kind of life?). I am not arguing here for the authenticity of claims about near-death experiences, but use this example to demonstrate that we need not think about our lives in an exclusively biological way. In our culture it is sometimes difficult to acknowledge any other purposes in life than to look young, make lots of money, and always be comfortable. This exclusive focus on matters of *bios* causes us to ignore the spiritual and psychological dimensions of life.

Many adults have a vague sense of being hollow people. Could it be because the *zoe* kind of life has been neglected? A book published some years ago was titled *It Takes a Long Time to Become Young*. What a great title and observation! Or, as someone else we remember said, "'Unless you change and become like little children you will never enter the kingdom of Heaven'" (Matthew18:3).

# "My Kids Aren't Very Interested in Church"

OVER THE YEARS I'VE heard many concerned parents of adolescents and young adults lament the fact that their children are not interested in church. Their young seem to have self-centered values, resist going to church, have only the other sex on their mind, and find religion boring. When they enumerate such symptoms, I can't help thinking how the same symptoms also apply to some "adolescents" who are thirty, forty, or fifty years of age.

What can be said to such concerned parents? I first like to remind them that these young people are normal. The late teens and early twenties are the least religious period of life. A lot is going on inside humans at this time. The healthy development of individuality is progressing, and during this time teenagers and young adults pull away from their parents and their parents' values, customs, preferences of dress, and so on. Although sometimes this is done in excess, the process itself is a healthy one; we humans are not made to stay in the nest all our life. We must become the unique person God made us to be. As youth clumsily try to fly on their own, they make a lot of mistakes. They fall on their faces at times, but fly they must. It calls upon the skills of good parents to know how much freedom to allow at this time, and when to step in to keep their young from hurting themselves as they grope for independence.

Spirituality is an important area of life, and it, too, is involved in this crucial time of adolescent growth and development. Young people are gradually moving from a secondhand faith to a firsthand faith. A secondhand faith is one we believe and follow only because someone else we love and respect holds and chooses it. Firsthand faith is a faith we choose and follow because of our own personal convictions. The hope of parents should be that their children will eventually come to believe firsthand in God and also embrace the religion they themselves practice and find full of meaning.

However, the move from a secondhand faith to a firsthand faith requires a period of questioning, re-examining, and even (for some people) apparently rejecting the secondhand faith. During this time of re-evaluating, it is important that young people see healthy religious habits lived out by their parents, and have someone of competence and wisdom to whom they can turn for solid spiritual and scriptural insights. The most helpful thing parents can do at this time of questioning is live their faith authentically and be prepared calmly to discuss why they believe what they believe.

Aside from personal witnesses and insightful discussions, young searchers need two other crucial components to arrive at a firsthand faith—time and suffering. A priest who is also a university professor was giving a presentation at a local parish one day. A worried mother asked him why her children seemed so uninterested in spiritual matters. He responded, "They haven't lived long enough or suffered enough." Sometimes we expect our children to be where we are. Yet we have only arrived at our convictions after the wear and tear of life, and as the grace of God has gradually formed us, taught us, convinced us. The passing of time as we grow and mature, and the sufferings we meet along the way, are great teachers. They accomplish wonders with all but the most resistant. Knowledge gradually becomes wisdom, searching yields to finding, and secondhand faith becomes firsthand faith.

# PART TWO

# Enrolled in the School of Life

# Celebrities and Heroes

IT'S MUCH HARDER TO BE a hero than a celebrity. Being a celebrity flows right along with our most satisfying natural desires. From birth we all like to be approved, applauded, and recognized as special. These desires come from the immediate needs of our ego. They are normal and understandable.

The way to celebrityhood is usually through qualities of the body. Coordination, speed, strength, beautiful looks, and musical talent are some of the stepping stones to celebrity in the United States. These qualities can make us a popular, wealthy, much-applauded person.

Sometimes we confuse being a celebrity with being a hero, but the two are quite different. Being a hero usually requires going *against* our natural desires. It means giving of ourselves to achieve the harder, higher, more altruistic goals that lie deep within us. For example, we all have a natural desire for self-preservation, to look out for our own life before that of all others. But when a soldier risks his life to save a combat buddy, or a woman braves a strong current to swim and save a drowning person, they go against their natural instinct and make the hard choice of risking themselves for the good of another. Whereas the source of celebrity is the talents of the body, the source of heroism is the exquisite talents of the heart and soul, the talents of love, integrity, selflessness, altruism, and courage.

Back in the 1980s, a commercial flight crashed into the Potomac River. Helicopters rushed to lift injured survivors out of the cold water before they drowned. One helicopter pilot recounted hovering over four people clinging to one another and some wreckage

49

in the river. He noticed that one of the men was partially bald. The helicopter lowered a rope and collar that could only carry to safety one person at a time. As the rope was lowered, the pilot noticed each time that the bald-headed man would grab it, but would wrap it around someone else instead of himself. After lifting the other three persons to shore, the helicopter returned finally for the caring man who had helped each of the others—but he was gone. His strength had evidently given out, and he had drowned. That man was a hero, not a celebrity.

Extolling heroes over celebrities doesn't mean that celebrities are awful people. It just means that being a celebrity is not nearly as demanding as being a hero. Although both affect a culture, heroes mean more to a society than do celebrities. Heroes' actions call us to emulate higher ideals.

We seem to have no shortage of celebrities today, but we need also to recognize our everyday heroes. We need to notice those people who go against societal pressures, easy instinct, greed, and self-centeredness to aim for higher goals such as love, the common good, genuine welfare of others, or patriotism. We need to acknowledge those who choose a particular behavior because it is right and uplifting or helps another, and not because it will get them money, fame, power, or status. There are recognizable heroes, like the man in the plane crash, and quiet heroes. Many quiet heroes are never known. Mothers and fathers who go against the natural desire for their own comfort and choose instead the growth and good of their children; people in business who forgo lucrative deals that are unjust; students who refuse to cheat on their exams or spouses who refuse to cheat on each other—they are all heroes.

Celebrities attract us to themselves; heroes attract us toward goodness and caring for others. Celebrities give autographs; heroes give the powerful example that we all have the potential for greatness within our heart.

# The Line That Runs Through Society

A LINE RUNS THROUGH society. It is an extremely important line, for it creates the moral climate in which we live. On one side of the line is what we consider ethical and appropriate behavior; on the other side of the line is what we consider immoral and destructive behavior. On one side is what we deem sacred, valuable, and beautiful, and on the other side what is vulgar, base, and demeaning.

It is a movable line. It can be, and actually is, moved by the people of a society. If we pull that line too tight, we restrict and suffocate ourselves; we become rigid, scrupulous, and unhappy people with little creativity, spontaneity, or joy. When the line is drawn close and tight, most human behavior is located on the other side of the line, where it is considered improper or immoral. Living becomes tedious and cautious.

If we push the line back too far, though, we also hurt ourselves. Then behavior previously considered immoral, unhealthy, and crass is allowed to surround us. Not much is considered sacred or valuable, baser instincts come to expression, and the aberrant behavior of many makes life more insecure for all.

Where, then, should we place that important line? An old Latin saying puts it well: *virtus stat in medio,* meaning "virtue stands in the middle." Finding that middle ground, where virtue stands, is the crucial endeavor of a society that seeks happiness.

Today many have an uneasy feeling that this important line has been pushed back too far. It has happened gradually over the past twenty-five years. Proponents of pulling the line in more tightly have met with accusations—that they are un-American, or in favor

51

of censorship and against personal rights. "This is a free country! I have my rights to say and do what I want," is a familiar cry. "What are you trying to do, ignore the Constitution and Bill of Rights?" As a result, few of us have objected, lest we be accused of being against progress and freedom or be identified as narrow religious zealots.

People of the United States have a confused notion of what freedom means. We think it means the ability to do what we want. That is not true! Freedom is the ability to do what we *ought;* license is the ability to do what we *want.* Sometimes what we want to do and what we ought to do are two very different things. I may like some of the nice things you own and want to take a few for myself, but I ought not do so—they are your property. Those oblivious to this distinction often equate responsibility with censorship. They find it hard to accept any curbs on the human ego and behavior.

Those who believe that we are creatures who come from the hand of God carry the conviction that there is a certain "oughtness" in our relationship with our Maker, that we ought to carry out the will of the One who made us. We are free to choose to do so or not, and the effects of our choices can be seen.

Society's ills indicate that we have made some poor choices and misused our freedom. We have been called a nation of sheep because most of us tend to be followers, not initiators. We let others seize the line and move it, while we say nothing. As a result, the line in our society is askew. We suffer in various ways, and our children's future will be affected. We are not a happy people as we prepare to enter the twenty-first century.

How can we begin to pull the line back to the middle? The strongest determinant of a society's line is the behavior and beliefs of its people. We must first look into our own heart. The line is established by human choices and decisions. How each of us lives has an impact on the placement of the line. Second, we must speak up and act with civility and reason when we perceive that the line is being negatively altered. Writing of our concerns in respectful but pointed letters to advertisers, members of Congress, television stations, and so on, often brings desired results. Using the power of our money, purchases, and personal vote also speaks loudly to many.

Tending the line is not the responsibility only of spiritually minded people. It is also the task of patriotic people who genuinely love their country. We can't ask God to bless America unless we do, too.

# Carpe Diem

MANY PEOPLE HAVE THE feeling they are chasing after something but not catching it. The "real thing" always seems to be happening somewhere else. When we're here, we think it's there; but when we get there, it has moved on to somewhere else. When we're young we think it will be when we get older and on our own, and when we get older we suspect it was when we were young. We're rarely satisfied with the present moment. We hurry past it to get somewhere else.

Yet it is in the present moment that our lives happen. Many of us have probably seen T-shirts and posters bearing that old Latin saying, *carpe diem*—"seize the day." It's an invitation to achieve fullness wherever we are, whatever our circumstances. Instead of cursing our situation, get into it in a healthful, wholesome sense. A mother who chauffeurs kids to ball practice and then stands on the sidelines can "lose the day" or "seize the day." She can lose it by feeling put-upon, thinking of the other places she would rather be, or the work being postponed by this seemingly futile task of being a chauffeur. Or she can seize the day by catching her breath and slowing down, enjoying the shapes of the trees, the laughter and enthusiasm of children, or the feeling of the breeze in her hair. Seizing the day, like all good things, requires effort on our part. It requires us to change gears from hurry to contentment, from worry to appreciation, from seeing life as ordinary to recognizing it as a miracle.

Sometimes the ability to seize the day does not come until we know our days are numbered. I have known terminally ill patients who, as their life ebbed away, were finally able to marvel at the simple beauty all around them, beauty that had been there all the while they hurried through life. They could be fascinated by a flock of birds all rising as one from a field, or thrill at the sound of the voice of someone they love coming down the hallway.

Every season, every day, has its own beauty. Put down the bad-news paper and turn off the television. Go for a walk or stand in the backyard noticing the feel of grass, or the buds that are swelling, the rustle of wind, the songbirds, or the lacy silhouette of winter trees without leaves. When our family or friends aren't aware that we are doing it, pause and look intently at their face and form, or some particular mannerism that is uniquely theirs. Can we see them anew as mysterious and wonderful people who have come into our lives, each possessing depth that calls out to be known? Do we ever realize that this is one of the good old days we'll look back on many years from now?

The more we are able to seize the day, the more we are seized by a deeper realization of how good life is. Settling more into the present moment adds worth to it, and reminds us that we can get so busy making a living that we forget to make a life.

# Seeking "Why" to Tolerate "What"

THE WORD *WHAT* IN THE title of this essay stands for any or all of the puzzling events of our lives. It means what happens to us, what comes our way, especially those events that are hard to understand. And any number of situations can come our way during a lifetime. There was the day my dog died; the time I flunked an important test; the moment I found out that my spouse was having an affair; the experience of my child's death; the time I failed to get a job I desperately needed; the day I was diagnosed with cancer. We all have our own lists, and they grow.

What comes our way is often understandable to us even though we don't like it; we see *why* it happened. I didn't get the job because the other applicant had more experience than I; my dog died because she was thirteen years old and past the usual lifetime for her breed; my spouse and I were fooling ourselves all these years—we never did really love each other or try that hard to build a relationship. Many of the painful events of our lives have a component to them that indicates the reason why they probably happened. And when we have a *why* we can better tolerate the *what*.

The most wrenching experiences are those that hurt us and seem to have no reason. Isn't the question "Why?" most commonly asked amid our pain and losses? Not only are we hurt and vulnerable, but we feel completely at the whim of chaos. A certain insanity seems afoot when creatures like ourselves, possessing the power of reason, come face-to-face with events that appear to have no reason. How can we expect to live our lives with some sense of equilibrium and security when chaos can happen at any time?

In looking for a *why,* it might help to consider these factors.

Perhaps there is a reason, a *why,* caused by us but that we don't see. We have an uncanny ability to build up defense mechanisms against reality. One of them is denial. We hide from reality. We sometimes deny and are oblivious to the very existence of the *why* we say we seek. Psychoanalysis or solid spiritual direction can often reveal this kind of *why.* For example, a man wondered why no one loved him, or ever found him interesting and worth staying with in a relationship. It was only after intense introspection with the help of a psychologist that he eventually saw the *why* within himself—that he kept people at a safe distance, staying superficial, and never really opening up and revealing himself. He discovered that he had a lot of work to do within himself, but he felt relieved because his loneliness, the *what* in his life, was not caused by some cruel God, insane fate, or heartless people, but by himself. When he grasped the *why,* he gained hope rather than feeling continued futility.

Perhaps on other occasions we don't see the *why* because we fail to acknowledge mystery. Many of us say we believe in God, but won't let God be God. We don't recognize God's will for us. We expect God to think as we do, follow our logic, and be grasped by our mind. In modern times we have lost the sense of mystery and replaced it with confidence in reason, technology, and science. We can solve the most complicated challenges of calculus and nuclear physics, and expect to similarly solve the mysteries of life and understand the mind of God. God, on the other hand, deals in paradoxes, apparent contradictions that amazingly turn out just right. Our inability to immediately answer the question *why* is often a step leading us into the mystery of God's way of doing things. Noble humans are often forged by the seemingly senseless struggles of life.

If we can ever believe in the mystery of a Divine Being who is well disposed toward us—even loves us dearly—then we don't have to know the *why* behind every *what* that happens. We can tolerate the ambiguity of not knowing because we trust in the greater mystery of a love that guides our lives. We trust a God who can write straight even with crooked lines.

# Our Illusions About Evil

MOST OF US LIVE WITH A huge funnel over our head. Because of our ability to collect and dispense news swiftly, all the world's hurts, tragedies, and natural disasters are gathered daily and dumped into the top of that funnel. We turn on our televisions or pick up the newspaper, and they all come falling out onto our head. And the worst of this news has made us so well acquainted with evil that we are in danger of being desensitized to it.

Not long ago a man in Dunblane, Scotland, walked into a school. He pulled out guns and shot and killed sixteen innocent five- and six-year-olds and their teacher. The headmaster's accurate assessment was, "Evil visited our school today." In our era of political correctness, when everything has a euphemistic name, it is realistic, but rare, to hear a direct acknowledgment that evil still exists. Because we have constructed three major illusions about evil, it is beneficial, perhaps even radical, to state that some human actions are wrong—dead wrong.

Our first illusion about evil is that it is exciting, fun, even desirable. We harbor the erroneous supposition that the really thrilling things of life are always off-limits. We feel that they have been arbitrarily placed there by stern authorities who live stunted lives. Remember the old saying, "Everything I want to do is either illegal, immoral, or fattening"? First parents, then organized religion and God are looked upon as enormous wet blankets dampening the pleasures we want to enjoy. From this perspective, we deny the existence of evil, or at least consider its definition to be a matter of opinion.

57

But once in a while something huge and grotesque occurs that shakes our conclusions about evil. The murders in Scotland, terrorist bombings, or recalling the Holocaust powerfully remind us of the ugliness of sin and evil.

Evil exists on a spectrum. Sometimes we need to see evil at its starkest to remember that it also exists in realities like child and spousal abuse, greed, violence, and drugs. No, evil is not exciting, fun, or desirable; it brings destruction, hurt, and pain.

Our second illusion is seen in the way we place evil at a distance from ourselves. Scapegoating and projecting have gone on as long as humans have existed: Other people may perform evil actions, but not I. It is always those others, of that other race or culture, who are guilty. Aleksandr Solzhenitsyn, the Russian writer, once created a strong image of the ubiquity of evil. He depicted us as wanting to think that there are just a few evil people perpetrating all the wrongs of the world. And if we could only build a wall or a fence around them and set them off from the rest of us, things would be fine. But as soon as we begin to draw the line between the good and the bad, we discover that it runs right down through the middle of our own heart. Every one of us has the potential for goodness, seen in our compassionate, loving, self-sacrificing actions; and each of us has a darker side, capable of evil, sin, and cruelty. The story of our lives is the struggle between these two sides.

Our third illusion about evil is related to the second. We believe that to rid ourselves of evil all we need to do is pass laws or put people in jail. Some people definitely need to be put in jail and kept apart from the rest of society. However, one of the tenets common to most religions, and demonstrated by Solzhenitsyn, is that evil is operative within our nature; we have a tendency toward selfishness, pride, greed, lust, cruelty, and so on.

Evil is basically overcome, to the extent that it can be, from the inside, not the outside. The Judeo-Christian religions emphasize that we cannot do it alone. We need a messiah, a savior, to teach us, empower us, and help lift us to be our best selves. Our best efforts need to collaborate with God's in order to be effective. It takes more than better guns, additional FBI agents, or stiffer prison sentences.

The spiritual nature of humans must be acknowledged and fostered. When this is done adequately, the illusions we use to masquerade evil will melt away, and we will see it for what it is—something that destroys us, our happiness, and our highest potential.

# If Only . . .

ONE OF THE FIRST LESSONS in the art of living is to learn to cope with problems in a healthy way. In general, we are to face our problems courageously, work through them, and come out on the other side better developed than before. Ernest Hemingway put it like this: "The world breaks every one and afterward many are strong at the broken places."

Some of us, unfortunately, carry through life the impression that there aren't supposed to be any problems. We become agitated and anxious about problems because of the discomfort they cause, and we harbor additional anger because we have problems at all. This resentment proves that we have not yet learned one of the fundamentals in the art of spiritual living. Problems are not just inconveniences to be avoided or cursed, but mysteries to be lived. To avoid dealing with problems is to refuse to enroll in the School of Life.

We humans grow in stages from lesser to greater maturity. Problems are frequently the catalysts that nudge our growth along. We often realize this only in hindsight. We eventually recognize that we have become more established in our own individuality, more compassionate, more human and humble, because we have experienced our own difficult situations and struggles. We learn to accept the fact that we cannot separate our lives from the situations in which we live them. We cannot be a parent and then try to avoid all the problems of being a parent, or remain single and avoid the problems of living alone. The moment we try to do so, we become unrealistic and inauthentic. We start living an "if only" existence.

In an "if only" existence, we persist in the belief that we would be happy and free of problems, and be delightful people, "if only" something were different. If only I had a different spouse; if only I had a more understanding boss; if only I'd get a promotion; if only the people around me were more interesting; if only my health were better, my face and body more beautiful, my imperfections more controllable—then I would live a happy, fulfilled, useful life. In the meantime, we neglect the opportunities for growth and fulfillment that are found in our own situation and struggles here and now.

Living in an "if only" world turns us away from reality. We become professional dreamers who never wake up. We become experts at complaining because we cannot accept that we and our world are not perfect, that there are obstacles in our path. We never come to see problems as an integral part of life, as mysteries that are involved paradoxically in our development. We fail to appreciate what it means to be a human.

When we're "if only" people, we have the tendency to move a lot. We try and avoid hard times by moving from spouse to spouse, job to job, house to house, friend to friend, unconsciously searching for a problem-free situation. Our restless changing indicates that we are running from life, running from ourselves. We will never find ourselves and become all we can be by running. We can only discover and bring to birth our real selves by living life as fully and realistically as possible in the "now," not in the "if only."

# Finding the Pony in Life

TWO LITTLE BOYS WERE good friends. They shared many interests, but had very different basic personalities. One was a pessimist, the other an optimist. Most adults who knew the boys felt a kinship with the pessimistic boy, for by the time you're a full-fledged adult you've had your knocks, lost some dreams, and expect the worst to happen. Most of the adults worried about the optimistic boy. He seemed too naive. "He's sure going to have some rough times someday," the adults said.

One day some of these adults decided to teach the optimistic boy a lesson with their own brand of reality therapy. They arranged for the boys to take an outing in the country to visit a farm. The pessimist didn't want to go at first because of the long trip. The optimist was overjoyed because he imagined farms to be interesting places. According to the plan, the farmer eventually took the two boys into a barn containing a huge pile of manure, ten feet high. The stench was awful. The adults watched as the boys stood in front of the manure pile. The pessimistic boy cried, gagged, held his nose, and screamed, "Get me out of here, this is terrible, take me home!" The optimistic boy smiled, clapped his hands in joy, and said excitedly, "I know there's a pony in there somewhere!"

Studies in cognitive psychology and spirituality demonstrate the personal benefits of looking for ponies. We usually look for ponies when we're younger. But as life continues, we experience many kinds of losses, and by midlife we realize that many of our dreams will not be fulfilled. We become more negative, pessimistic, and cynical because we believe we deserve better. We stop looking for ponies. Besides, the life we read about in

61

newspapers and hear about on TV news constantly authenticates the manure piles all around us. Optimism becomes a challenge.

Amid this reality, how can we learn to clap our hands and look for ponies rather than hold our noses about life?

First, we can take control of our thoughts. The thoughts that constantly flit through our mind affect our moods and attitudes. When we are alone in the car, walking, waiting in line, and so on, we can step back from our thoughts and analyze them briefly. Are they negative in tone? Are we feeling sorry for ourselves, sad for what we don't have, remembering mistreatments? If they are negative, changing thoughts changes attitudes. We have the power to throw out negative thoughts and welcome positive ones. We can think of all that we have, of who loves us, of the beauty of nature, and of this day we are living, which has never been lived before. It is invigorating to feel our good fortune rather than focus on the feeling that we are victims. We can gradually make our life a more attractive color by controlling our thoughts and making sure we stay aware of the good we have.

Second, we can look at the bigger picture. Our lives are tapestries that are being woven. They are being woven by a provident God who loves each of us passionately. We're asked to trust this providence and even join in the weaving. We can't see the full picture yet. Today may be difficult, ambiguous, and puzzling, but when the picture is completed, everything will fit. When life is hard, we should be aware that such times need not make us bitter persons, but better persons. Seeing the bigger picture is a source of hope.

Finally, think of others. Navel gazing usually only convinces us that we have odd-shaped navels. Focusing too much on ourselves leads to an inner emptiness and discontent, whereas empathy for others does wonders. When miserable people came to a famous psychiatrist wanting to feel better, he would treat some of them. But to some his prescription would be, "Lock up your house, go down the street, and help somebody; get your mind off yourself." In parishes where I have served, some parishioners take Communion to hospital patients. Inevitably, they remark how much they are helped by visiting those who are sick. By giving ourselves away, we find ourselves. It seems that when life is piled ten feet high with unpleasantness, if we sincerely reach out to others, we find they hold the end of an invisible bridle and hand it to us—and it's connected to a pony.

# The Practice of Justice

PEOPLE TALK A LOT ABOUT virtues these days. One of the most important virtues is justice. There are many theological and legal definitions of *justice*. To put it simply, we can say that it means "fairness" or "rightness." A just person is a person who tries to treat everyone fairly, and expects to be treated that way, too.

Justice is an essential element in relationships and society. The human conscience (which, centuries ago, was called the *vox Dei,* or voice of God) enables us to recognize justice when we see it. There is a certain built-in "oughtness" or standard that we gradually develop if we mature normally. For example, if you earn some money and I stealthily take it away from you, a normally developed person instinctively realizes that was wrong. I ought not to have done that, and I ought to give the money back.

If justice is present to a significant degree in society, it promotes security, peace, and trust. If it is not present, the well-being of a community begins to disintegrate. People feel unsure, and fear and distrust escalate. Personal safety becomes the ultimate concern. A vague feeling grows that life is not right, and we feel powerless to change things.

The people of the United States are feeling uneasy these days. We have a vague feeling that things are not right, not fair, that justice is eroding. Yes, we know that life will never be completely fair, but we also know that fairness is a goal toward which we must struggle. For example, when alleged criminals are brought to trial, the public watches intently—and with televised courtroom proceedings, the attention given has increased. Many watch out of curiosity, perhaps reveling in the misfortune of others. But besides curiosity, people also have a deep desire to see if puzzling problems and complex crimes will come out fair and right—whether justice will be served. And it is in our own best interest that it does.

Right now we're growing less sure that justice prevails. Instead, it seems that injustice often prevails. We see criminals who are paroled too soon, victims who are forgotten, legal loopholes that allow escape, endless litigation, and money to be the key factor in getting away with crime. Justice often seems to have been replaced with the "virtue" of cleverness.

Whenever we discuss the ailments of a society, we need to realize that the healing process must start with each of us. Not only must we elect public officials of integrity and justice, but we must practice justice ourselves. I recently saw a man who did that very thing. He was in front of me in a supermarket checkout line. When the young cashier gave him his change, he counted it, counted it again, and said to her, "You gave me too much money." She thanked him and accepted back a ten-dollar bill.

Such a trivial example, you say? Yes, in a way. But that man was being something very important; he was being a just man. In that busy supermarket a number of people observed what happened. I'm sure some said to themselves, "He should have kept it; a big business like this will never miss ten bucks." Such people have muted consciences. Certainly other people saw what happened and appreciated the justice involved in his decision to give the money back. The money was not his, and he knew it. Perhaps his example will encourage others to do likewise. For when we are fair and just, our conscience, the *vox Dei,* quietly informs us, "You have done as you ought!"

# Where Did Love Go?

MANY LONG-MARRIED people wonder whether it is ever possible to regain the joyous, romantic, soul-deep love they once felt. They feel that what exists between them now as love is a tired, routine, lesser brand. So some couples divorce in order to try to find that feeling again with a different partner. Others conclude that love is an illusion. Still others close up shop emotionally and say, "If anything ever happens to my spouse, I don't think I'll get married again." An old proverb says, "Only the beginnings of love are beautiful." Is that right? Years ago, when first love bloomed, young hearts rolled and reveled in the clouds. Now, too many look up at the clouds and wish they could touch them again.

We have such a deep yearning for closeness and passion, for warm and tender love. We want to really matter to someone, and for them to matter to us, not just for a temporary affair, not for a year or two, but for always. However, as time goes by, the inverse seems true to many. Romance seems to cool, closeness becomes distance, sex becomes perfunctory, and the yearnings of the heart seem unanswered. Questions arise in the back of minds: "Should I stay?" "Has love ended?" "Did I even love in the first place?" "Can I, we, find our way back again to when it was beautiful?"

The rarest commodities of life are the most expensive. They cost us very much, sometimes more than we're willing to pay. Somewhere in adolescence, first love was just dropped into our lap. It was so thrilling and fortuitously given because we need strong encouragement at that age to let another person into our self-centered lives. Although we were very self-centered, we let the other person in— and we fell in love. That this love was immature is shown by the fact that the strongest encouragement to letting the other person into our lives was the pleasure they brought. The thrills of first love are free to us. But after that, they are a rare commodity and must be worked for. There comes a time when Santa Claus stops coming to our house.

For mature love to have similar thrills, we must risk a lot of ourselves. Most of all, we must work at communicating. Communicating doesn't mean chattering about inanities. It means opening up the deep recesses of our heart and mind to each other. It means revealing who we really are, our fears and hopes, our vulnerabilities, even though we realize at the same time that what we reveal could lead to our rejection. But unless we are truly known, we cannot be truly loved. If we ever hope to be deeply and warmly loved, we must uncover our true selves to the one we hope will love us. Our best hope is that the person we love will do the same, and that together we will accept and treasure what we see in each other.

Past generations did not put the premium on communication and emotional fulfillment that we do today. In the past, faithfully carrying out marital roles was the criterion for calling a marriage a success. The emphasis on communication is a positive change, but today we are perhaps too quick to deem our marriage a failure if we do not always feel emotionally and psychologically fulfilled. The pain of feeling unfulfilled is not necessarily the sign of failure—it is often a natural nudge to remind us that it will take more work and communication to move on to a deeper stage of love. It is unfortunate when the feeling of a lack of fulfillment is immediately taken as a sign that "it's over."

The busyness of life, economic expectations, the unchecked buildup of resentments, and the raising of children make it very difficult for married couples to communicate with regularity and quality. Communication also tends to diminish through the years because we think we know all there is to know about the other, or we hesitate to bring up emotion-laden topics. Yet the memory of first love keeps whispering in our heart and dares to suggest that later love can be even deeper and richer. An illusion? No! I've met too many long-married lovers to know that it's true.

# Unhealthy Rescues

TO RESCUE A DROWNING man, to pull a woman from a burning car, to grab a child about to run into traffic, to carry a wounded soldier out of the line of fire—these are examples of admirable acts of rescue. Some can even be called heroism. However, to hide a bottle of liquor from an alcoholic to diminish temptation, to do tomorrow's homework for a child who has ignored it all week, to give free lodging to a healthy relative who cannot hold a job, to repeatedly forgive a violent husband in order to save him from embarrassment or prosecution—these and countless other situations are examples of unhealthy rescue. Superficially, we may feel we are being kind and helping someone. Realistically, we are often hurting them by subtly confirming their lack of responsibility and personal growth.

Healthy rescues occur when we give or risk ourselves, our time, our resources, or our safety for people who are in jeopardy despite all their best efforts to help themselves. Unhealthy rescues try to do for others what they can and must learn to do for themselves. Some people, resistant to the discomfort involved in growing up, often remain like babies and "milk" the kindness of others. They learn early in life what kind of manipulation works to get us to do things for them. They may cry out to be rescued by feigning sickness, helplessness, or ignorance; by threatening to withhold their love; by berating themselves; by seeking to instill guilt in us if we don't help. They'll do anything to get someone else to rescue them in their current dilemma. Their cries for our help are not rare occurrences for them. Rather, this becomes a pattern, a modus operandi or "way of working." Parents, friends, or spouses, if

67

they do not realize what's going on, often step in and keep coming to the rescue. Their well-intentioned but misguided love leaves them feeling cruel or harsh if they don't always rescue when the call comes.

True, refusing to respond to unhealthy rescue pleas may seem cruel at first. However, real love sometimes demands exercising what is called "tough love"—tough because it is hard for both the one being asked for help and the one seeking rescue. But when we truly love someone, we want them to become the mature adults they are called to be. We think beyond the moment, to a lifetime. Our task sometimes involves challenging them to develop and become aware that they are chiefly responsible for their own life.

It's a strange twist in personal dynamics, but when one person too often tries to rescue and help another, resentment grows toward the one who does the helping. The person we help may be pleased for the moment, but he or she eventually comes to hate the rescuer. On a deep level, rescue insults the person's maturity and potential. It implies, "You are a weak, pitiable person who can't handle the challenges of your own life." This deep insult is the source of resentment.

Most of us would do anything we can to rescue the people we love from their problems when we see that their need is genuine. That's admirable. However, we must also be wise lovers, knowing when to rescue and when to encourage others to grow and be responsible for themselves.

# Feeling Good About Feeling Bad

THE TITLE OF THIS ESSAY may give the impression that it is about masochism, but that is not the topic at hand. Rather, the title refers to the strange fact that there are times in life when we may feel bad, but, if we are astute enough, we can see the positive side of whatever it is that is making us feel bad. Some examples may say it better.

There was a mother who got along well with her thirteen-year-old daughter. They shared personal conversations and in general enjoyed each other's company. Slowly the daughter began to change. One day, the mother was going shopping, an activity they had often enjoyed together. As she was about to leave for the mall, she passed through the family room and asked her daughter, "Linda, I'm going to the mall; want to come along?" The daughter looked up soberly and said, "No! What made you think I'd want to do that?"

The mother, who was well versed in psychology, felt bad but realized as she drove alone to the mall that important inner changes were going on in her daughter's life—changes leading to greater individuality and independence. And though she felt bad about the growing distance between her daughter and herself, the psychological insights she possessed enabled her also to feel good that her daughter was maturing normally. Without this awareness, a lot of harsh and insensitive words could have passed between them, as well as attempts to stymie the natural process of growth. The mother was smart to allow herself to feel good about feeling bad.

Let's consider another example. In the moments before wedding ceremonies, I've seen grooms become extremely nervous as the time approached. Some sneaked out to their car or had a friend supply them with alcohol to try to get rid of the anxiety. Those who did so were not wise enough to realize that feeling bad was really a good sign. They were about to take one of the most important steps of their life—making a lifelong commitment to live as husband and wife. Their nervousness was a subtle and deep realization of the seriousness of the crucial vow they were about to make. It is understandable that they would be apprehensive right before such a monumental decision. Should they expect to feel casual, as though nothing much were happening, or not to feel some anxiety about such an important choice? With a proper understanding, such grooms can certainly feel good about feeling bad.

What we consider hard or apprehensive is not necessarily bad. We live in a "feel good" society that says in so many ways, "If you're experiencing a troublesome, unpleasant feeling, then drug it away, drink it away, distract yourself by work, or do something to avoid thinking about it." A commercial for a pain medication encouraged us to purchase it by proclaiming, "I haven't got time for the pain." We fail to see that some wonderful things can cause a healthy angst in us, and that a process of growth may be occurring at the same time.

It seems like a strange twist to say that sometimes we can feel good about feeling bad. But it's true. Realizing it doesn't take the bad away, but it puts it into the larger context of the growth that is taking place in our lives. It helps us look at some of our bad feelings in a new way, cope with them more effectively, and appreciate this mysterious process we call life.

# The Reasons for Our Loneliness

I'LL NEVER FORGET THE words of one of my college psychology professors. He was discussing human relationships. He drew a little stick figure on the blackboard, then put circles around it, each new circle a little farther out, like the rings we see in a tree trunk after it has been cut down. The circle nearest the stick figure in the center was circle number one, then two, three, and so on.

He said we all have circles of friends. Some friends are in circle five, some in circle four, or eight, and so on, depending on how much we mutually share of our real selves and feelings, how much we trust each other, and the quality of our personal connection. Most of our friends are in various outer circles. The first circle of friendship holds that person with whom we can share our deepest thoughts and feelings, good and bad—and she or he is able to share the same with us. Then came the professor's statement I've remembered ever since. He said, "If, in your lifetime, you have one or two people in that first circle, consider yourself lucky!"

In the camaraderie of high school and college we think we'll have numerous first-circle friends forever. When we get older, we realize otherwise. In fact, one of the most common human feelings is loneliness. Everyone knows how loneliness feels.

Our loneliness comes from three sources. First, we are responsible for some of it. We probably have personal traits that are not likable to others, just as others have traits that do not appeal to us. That's life. Behaviors like self-centeredness, insensitivity, or unwillingness to risk true communication may also discourage potential friends. We hunger

71

for the closeness of a first-circle friend (especially in a spouse), but we often keep them at a distance by our defenses and fears. We may not offer understanding and acceptance when they share their deep feelings and thoughts, so they cease doing so. We may also drive people away by clinging to them with a sort of dependent desperation that demands, "Make me happy!"

But in addition to the loneliness we cause ourselves, there is a second kind of loneliness that comes to every human just by being human. It is a great burden that comes from a great glory. The great glory is our uniqueness—there is no one exactly like us. Being one of a kind causes an existential loneliness. We have much in common as human beings, yet each of us is a separate person with our own collection of hereditary, experiential, and personal factors that will never be repeated. That makes each of us so gloriously special—and so individually alone. We spend our lives trying to reconcile this loneliness by bridging the distance between ourselves and others. We search for that rare someone— sometimes called a soul mate—who will recognize our glorious uniqueness, understand and accept us, and let us see his or her uniqueness.

We need to be realistic, however, and acknowledge the continual work required to achieve the closeness we seek. We must struggle, be humble, communicate, risk, and forgive again and again. All the while, we look for the same from that potential first-circle friend. But it's all worth it. Some of the deepest joys of life are found, and much loneliness dispelled, if we ever develop that first-circle relationship with another human.

Yet, all of our loneliness can never be dispelled. If we think it can, all friends and spouses will disappoint us. For a spiritually wise person knows that there's a third kind of loneliness that will never be totally overcome by any other human. It's the loneliness caused by our destiny to be with our greatest friend of all. It was aptly expressed by Saint Augustine centuries ago when he said this about our yearning for God: "You have made us for yourself, and our heart is restless until it rests in you."

# Forgive and Forget?

FORGIVE AND FORGET—somewhere along the way we began to link the two terms together. It is an inaccurate linkage. Everything that happens to us becomes part of us. We cannot forget parts of ourselves. Some people seem to forget. If some of the events of our lives are very traumatic and too painful to think about, a psychological process pushes them underground, often beyond memory. It's called repression. We've all read of cases of adults forgetting terrible things that their parents or others did to them when they were children. The tragic event slips beyond conscious awareness and lies fathoms deep. Repression serves an immediate purpose, but psychologists tell us that it is not good for our mental health. The most productive thing to do is to meet our demons and deal with them. Often we need a competent professional to help us do so.

Most of our hurts are not traumatic. They come from family, friends, and colleagues in our daily living.

Although we cannot forget the hurtful things people do to us, we are called upon to forgive them. Forgiveness is often misunderstood. It doesn't mean acting as if some hurtful thing never happened, or that it was actually all right, or no big deal. Forgiveness does not mean forcing ourselves to like the person who hurt us. How can we like a molester or a hateful person? How can we like a parent or former spouse who used, abused, or severely mistreated us? Liking a person means that our emotions are favorably disposed toward her or him. Sometimes, after being hurt, that will never again be humanly possible.

73

Forgiveness, however, is a different matter. Forgiveness does not flow from our emotions but from our will, our choice. We can forgive only if we acknowledge the hurt, not if we pretend it never happened. We can forgive someone with the full awareness that we will never like them. Forgiving requires a lot from a person. It requires us to try to understand, not like, the person who hurt us. To understand them, we need to be aware that although they are responsible for their actions, they may have psychological or spiritual problems, or are emotionally undeveloped and ignorant of the harmful effect of their actions or words. Perhaps they are very self-centered or even hateful persons, and that blinds them to the feelings of others. And although we can never forget what they did, we make a decision to forgive what they did, set it aside, and refuse to keep chewing it over and over again in our heart.

Why be forgiving? For several reasons. First, because God forgives *us*. If we believe in a God who created us and loves us, we know that we ourselves need God's forgiveness many times, sometimes for very serious moral offenses. Second, if we cannot forgive others, we usually find it difficult to experience ourselves as forgiven by God, and we have difficulty forgiving ourselves. This leads us to maintain a certain rigid severity toward others and ourselves. Finally, without forgiveness we miss that special feeling of starting over again. Forgiving and making up, when possible, is a most enjoyable experience for both people involved.

In the course of a lifetime, we all have plenty of opportunities to forgive. Our parents, our children, our spouse, our brothers and sisters, our friends and colleagues, and ourselves are not flawless and perfect. In varying ways, we all fail, are petty or hateful at times; we all say and do things we regret, or should regret if we're honest enough. We don't have to look far to see a need for forgiveness.

Forgiving is not only spiritually appropriate, it is psychologically helpful. Forgiving frees us. It frees us from being small, vindictive, hateful persons who see ourselves as perpetual victims. It opens an interpersonal channel that was clogged. It lifts us up a notch to a certain nobility of character that comes from love, courage, and the willingness to reach for higher, healthier goals.

Forgetting is humanly impossible. Forgiving is extremely hard, but possible, and godlike. We all need forgiveness at times. But if we cannot reach out and forgive, we destroy the very bridge across which we ourselves must pass.

# How
# Do
# You
# Love
# Me?

ON THE BLACK VELVET CLOTH lie three beautiful diamonds. They all glisten in the light; they are all cut precisely. But are they all diamonds? No, one is glass, one zircon, and one an actual diamond. They range in value from twenty dollars to several thousand. An ordinary person would have a hard time telling them apart, but a professional gemologist could tell immediately.

Let's look at three possible kinds of love that are set before us. They seem to look alike, but need to be carefully distinguished. We'll call the first kind "if" love. It's the most common type. It glitters and glistens, but it's not very valuable. This kind of love is ego-centered and offered only in exchange for something our lover wants from us. "If you meet my expectations and be the way I want you to be, I'll love you." "If you do what I want, and accept any kind of treatment from me, I'll love you." "If you live up to my idea of what a spouse should be, I'll love you." Or the adolescent bargain, "If you date me and have sex with me, I'll love you." Many relationships, even marriages, break apart because they are built on "if" love. Eventually, expectations are not met and disillusionment sets in. Then what was formerly thought of as love turns into disinterest or hate.

Sometimes even parental love can be tainted by "if" love. Children sometimes receive the impression that to be loved, to be the pride and joy of their parents, they have to meet a lot of expectations and act a certain way. They hear, although not in so many words, "If you behave and do well in school, we'll love you." They sense that they are not loved just because of who they are, but for

75

how well they obey or what they accomplish. Such children become adults who go through life with a searching sadness. They are still looking for someone to love them just for themselves.

A second kind of love could be called "because" love. One person claims to love another because of a quality the other possesses, something she or he has, or something she or he does. "I love you because your body is so beautiful." "I love you because you are so popular or rich, powerful or well known." "I love you because you have a convertible and are so romantic." "I love you because you're sought by so many others." This kind of love seems a little better than "if" love at first, but after a while it, too, becomes a burden. If we are loved "because" of a quality we have, what happens if we lose that quality, or if someone else comes along who has more of it?

If we sense that "because" love is the basis of our relationship with another, insecurity results. We're afraid that we might not really be the lovable person our lover thinks we are. We become fearful and try never to appear to have lost the tenuous quality that endears us to the one we want. For if the quality goes, will love go too?

The third kind of love is unconditional love. We could also call it "in spite of" love. It is different from "if" love because it has no expectations; it expects nothing in return. It is different from "because" love in that it is not brought forth by a quality we possess or things we have. In unconditional love, we are loved "in spite of," not "because of." We do not deserve it or earn it, we just receive it as a tremendous gift. This is the kind of love for which our hearts are desperately hungry, yet it is a very rare gem to find. It does genuine wonders for our esteem. Fortunate are those who experience it. It is the way God loves us.

# Words in Sheep's Clothing

WE ARE ALL FAMILIAR with the concept of a "wolf in sheep's clothing," in which hostile intent is disguised with friendly behavior. One of the more popular games we adults play could be called "*Words* in Sheep's Clothing." In this game, we try to hide harsh realities from ourselves and others by giving them pleasant- or inoffensive-sounding names, or euphemisms. At the death camp Treblinka, the Nazis called the barbed-wire-lined path leading to the gas chamber *die Himmelstrasse,* which means "the road to heaven." In France, an abortionist is sometimes referred to as an "angel maker." "Adult" bookstores offer sexually explicit material to people whose psychosexual development is often childish.

Our use of euphemisms not only attempts to hide harsh realities, it also attempts to exonerate us from responsibility. We often justify self-centered and irresponsible actions by referring to them as aspects of our "freedom" or "rights." Listen closely to the words used when we speak of situations in which irresponsibility is involved. For example, a TV program about unmarried teen parents showed a picture of a young woman of eighteen who had two children. The narrator said, "She was only sixteen when she found herself pregnant with her first child." "Found" herself pregnant? That sounds very much like she was completely passive and surprised one day by life.

In the same program, the narrator described a twenty-six-year-old man who had five children: "His first child came along when he was only a sophomore in high school, and he has been struggling ever since." His first child "came along"! Such language tends to mask the reality of cause and effect and excuses us from taking personal responsibility for our actions.

Noticing the word choices of others is revealing, but it's especially helpful to notice our own. It serves as an exercise in self-analysis and offers surprising insights. How many times do we claim that someone "made us" angry? That choice of words exonerates us from poorly moderating our own emotions. How many times do we prefer to say we're "too busy" when our spouse asks for some quality time, rather than admit that we find it difficult to carry on solid communication? No one will blame us for working hard, and that is the sheep's clothing that hides our unwillingness to deal with important relational issues.

Assessing our words is not a useless pastime. To the psychologically astute person, our choice of words, slips of the tongue, assignments of blame, and so on, really say a lot about ourselves. If we are honest and pay close attention to the way we express ourselves, we get a truer picture of ourselves and can make some significant steps in personal growth and understanding.

If we go through life putting sheep's clothing on our words and actions, we become more and more distant from reality and our true selves. Doing so may fool others, but we wind up fooling ourselves and being consumed by the wolf within.

# Listening

WE LIVE IN A WORLD OF wall-to-wall words. Radio and TV programs, billboards, commercials, talk shows, telephones, cellular phones, computers, the Internet, movies, Walkmans, solicitors, politicians—all join in making sure each of us gets an abundant dose of words. Chattering is common, substance is rare, empathy almost nonexistent. And as the amount of words increases, our ability to really listen decreases.

Stopping ourselves from listening to the world at large is a protective mechanism. It salvages our personal thoughts and lets us catch our "auditory breath," as it were. But it can also have negative consequences. Some people have perfected "nonlistening" to an art. While we talk, they can look in our eyes, smile and nod occasionally, say, "Oh," and shake their heads knowingly—but they are really far away or thinking of what to say next. We get so used to turning off the barrage of hype and commercial words that we also begin to turn off the communication that needs to exist between us and people with whom we want to be close.

Not listening helps create lonely people. Someone once said of writers that we write to prove that we are not alone. We write hoping that someone is going to read our writing and, in a sense, listen to us, connect with us. We all speak (or write) for the same reason. Whenever we use words, we are really trying to tell our story, little pieces about ourselves, who we are, and what's inside this mystery called "me." But we do so cautiously, unconsciously hiding the true impact of words. We're afraid that people might not like what they learn about us. So it takes careful listening to hear what someone else is really saying, and who is behind the words and the sound. For example, a child who says, "I don't love you" may really be saying, "I'm angry at you for not giving me what I want," or questioning whether he or she is really loved.

When we don't listen well to each other, a connection is missed. And when connections are missed, our story goes unheard and our feelings unperceived; we begin to conclude that we are not worth listening to and are all alone in a large cacophonous crowd.

Three groups who often feel they are not listened to are children, spouses, and elderly people. We presuppose the words of children to be frivolous, the words of our spouse predictable, and the words of the elderly irrelevant. Out of hunger to be listened to and taken seriously, children may demonstrate asocial behavior, spouses may seek another heart, and elderly people may tend to dwell in the past, reliving productive times that said "I was somebody."

One of the greatest gifts we can give to another is to look into their eyes, and, with undivided attention, really listen to what they say. We instinctively know when someone is not listening, and we feel slightly cheapened by the encounter. On the other hand, we also know when someone else genuinely listens. We feel a connection, we sense an empathy that implies, "You matter to me; you and your life are worth knowing."

A friend of mine once laughed and spoke of his dislike of going to high school or college reunions. He said, "A reunion is a time when people you once knew shake your hand and say 'hi' and other kind words, but all the while they're looking over your shoulder to see who else is there." Many people feel that way about life. So, do you want to give a wonderful gift to people you love? Listen. Listen with your heart!

# Just Because We Can, Does It Mean We May?

SOME THIRTY YEARS AGO, I read a fascinating book titled *Come, Let Us Play God.* The author, Leroy Augenstein, was then chairman of the department of biophysics at Michigan State University and a member of the Michigan State Board of Education.

Augenstein's point was that our technological, scientific, and medical advancements have outpaced our moral and ethical competency. We have learned how to do many amazing things. But whenever we deal with matters like heart transplants, the ability to detect birth defects, in vitro fertilization, methods of prolonging or ending the life of the elderly or comatose, genetic engineering, and so on, we are also faced with the necessity of making value judgments. We have many more such options now than when Augenstein wrote his book, and will have even more as time goes on.

However, humans are moral beings. We have a conscience, can experience guilt, and, from the time we are very young, we are increasingly aware that some things are right and some things are wrong. Most of us believe in an all-knowing Creator God who has a plan for creation. We can try to ascertain God's plan by studying our nature, our responsibilities to one another and the common good, and, as best we can determine, the will of God. We base our choices on these factors.

Questions arise as a result of our technological and scientific advances on the one hand, and our nature as moral beings on the other. Just because we can do something, does that mean we may?

With the modern emphasis on individual rights, many bristle at such a question: "What do you mean, may I do something? I'll do it if I want, I have my rights." Such an attitude ignores those other critical factors such as the implications of our nature, the common good, and the will of God. It usurps the place of God and places only self-interest at the center of decision making. Such an attitude is too simplistic, and in error.

The ethical issues with which we struggle can be staggering. If I discover through current medical techniques that my unborn baby has Down's syndrome, or is not the gender I want at this time, and because civil law permits and medical techniques make it possible, may I abort the diseased or unwanted child? Medical tests can now confirm whether we have latent diseases that will eventually appear and shorten our life. Should we take the test? Then, if we discover that we have a latent, life-shortening disease, are we to tell our fiancé or spouse? Are we to have children to whom we might pass it on? If we discover that one person has a latent disease and another person does not, does that make the one person worth more than the other? May a government, employer, or life insurance company force us to take a complete medical exam and then reveal the complete results? May we engage in genetic engineering? May we end the life of someone who is suffering but not dying?

Thousands of such scenarios are possible today. All can be reduced to the question, Just because we can do something, does that make it moral and proper? How are we to decide the morality of these scenarios?

Too many people try to decide such complex issues by depending on their emotions and how they feel about it. Few read about complex moral issues other than in popular magazines; few seek out the counsel of competent people, or discuss and digest theological or ethical considerations. Larger guiding principles are often unknown, unsought, or misunderstood. Rather than reflect and develop our thoughts, we often just base our opinions on the results of polls.

If we can do something, may we? Well, if we're God, yes. If we're a creature of God's, then accountability is involved. We can't just play God. An advanced technological and scientific age needs ethically advanced people.

# Meeting
# Our
# Demons

DO YOU READ IN THE PAPER about all the gross and gory things people do? Have you noticed that man on the TV news who's on trial for what he did to that little girl? Or heard about the woman who was drunk and drove into the crowd at the bus stop? See Dick, see Dick run, and shoot, or steal, or hurt his wife, or pull a shady business deal!

Most people who do hurtful or evil things do so because they have not faced their demons. We seek desperately for excuses. He didn't take his Prozac that day; his father left home when he was a small child; her family was rich and gave her everything but real love, and so on. Listen to the cases prepared by defense lawyers and you'll witness the grasping and reaching for excuses. Sure, various factors affect people and predispose them to unhealthy behavior. Those factors have to be reasonably weighed in the light of truth. But today's modus operandi is often "the devil made me do it!" Somebody, something, someone else is responsible for my behavior, not me. Not me and my pet demon.

All of us have demons. By demons I mean some personal weakness, some subtle but strong tendency toward selfishness, greed, lust, cruelty, hate, anger, self-righteousness, or any one of a hundred other moral flaws. I have been living with myself too long and have heard too many confessions to suffer from the illusion that some humans are free of demons. They are part of our imperfect nature.

We need to come to know our demons and do battle with them. Many of us do not. One of the reasons I have always admired faithful members of Alcoholics Anonymous is that they have acknowledged their demon.

Every week they go to one or more meetings facing up to that which would tear their life apart. But for every person who comes and fights, there are five others, absent, who keep fooling themselves that they have no demon.

Misuse of alcohol is an obvious demon. Most demons go unacknowledged. Seeing them would demand more honesty than we want. Sometimes ignorance can help our self-image. The successful businessman whose demons are the materialism and greed that goad him into forgoing healthy family relationships for the sake of money; the parent whose demon is a selfish nature that cares little about her children and all the personal effort involved in raising them well; the clergyman whose demon urges him to be so cocksure of his own rightness he becomes cold and rigid and looks down his holy nose at others—these are some of the secret demons running amok. Their owners deny that they exist. That way the struggle can be avoided.

While I ask myself, may I ask you—what is your demon? In your heart of hearts, what weakness most rules your life? What's been around for such a long time it's almost like a familiar pet? What excuses do you use to avoid struggling with your demon? Whom do you blame for it being there? Do you envision yourself ever doing anything about it? When will that be, and what will you do? Whatever you plan to do, are you aware that it will take the greatest courage, the most patience, and be the hardest endeavor you ever began? Demons don't die easily.

And do you know what will become of you if you ever control or conquer your demon? You will experience an exhilarating freedom. You, and I, want so much the freedom to be our real, true self, don't we? We are only living part of our lives when something else is in charge. If you want to go for this freedom and a better sense of self, something's got to go. So meet it, beat it!

# The Pleasure of Being Angry

A CERTAIN PLEASURE OR benefit can be attached to anger. Although long-lasting anger takes its toll, gnawing away at concentration, serenity, and creativity, we enjoy a certain aspect of it; for all the while we are feeling angry, we are also feeling righteous and superior. Someone else has been at fault, wronged me, or acted stupidly. At times anger is an appropriate, natural feeling.

Anger is also a feeling that masks other feelings more distressing to our egos. For example, a young man and his girlfriend had been going together for most of high school. As they reached the end of their senior year, it became evident that their desire for different careers meant that they would be attending universities more than a thousand miles apart. They graduated and began the final summer months together before they left for college. However, sometime during the summer they had an argument. Rather than resolving it in their usual way, they remained distant, cool, and angry. "I'm sure glad I found out how selfish he really is," she thought. "I didn't know she could be so unreasonable and unforgiving," he said. When they left for college, their anger toward each other remained, so they turned their attention to making new friends in their new surroundings.

Sounds like an ordinary situation, doesn't it? Yet there is a good possibility that they were using their unresolved argument and lingering anger in a subtle, unrecognized way. After a long and happy a relationship throughout high school, parting would have been so very difficult. At such times, feelings of sadness, loss, and emptiness wrench our heart and make us miserable. We feel so vulnerable, needy, depressed, and lonely at times like this.

So what do we do at such times? Sometimes we unconsciously create an unpleasant situation in which we can become angry and stay angry. It is easier to leave angry than sad, to feel superior and wronged rather than needy and vulnerable. So we sink our teeth into anger, chew on it constantly in our mind, and create that self-stroking attitude that says, "I'm glad we parted!" Imagined gladness, born of anger, replaces sadness.

Holding on to anger can also have the unhealthy effect of protecting us from our wider humanness. Anger is just one of many human feelings. We are capable of feeling so much, like sadness, loneliness, nostalgia, need of others, tenderness, appreciation, gratitude, compassion, and love. When anger is our chief emotion, we shield ourselves from the fullness of being human. We impoverish ourselves. We save our egos from the pain associated with many emotions, but lose a lot of the other essential positive elements of human life also associated with our emotions. Anger can consume our mind, our physical health, other emotions, and our experience of life. Anger can eat us alive.

Resolving anger by understanding and forgiveness is crucial for a happier life. We like to think we are doing others a favor by forgiving them, yet the one for whom we are doing the biggest favor might just be ourselves. Anger is just another example of how important it is to know ourselves well.

Anger is prevalent these days. We see it in traffic, at the supermarket, at the office, at school, at athletic events, and in interpersonal relationships. It is sometimes so intense that we might call it rage instead of anger. Its presence indicates that a lot of us have delicate and selfish egos all wrapped up in ourselves and resistant to self-knowledge and the joys and sorrows of being human. Life should make us understanding and compassionate, not angry. We'll stop hugging anger close to our heart the moment we realize our own fragility and learn to genuinely hug and care for others.

# PART THREE

## The
## Seasons
## of
## Human
## Life

# Christmas and Yearning for Home

AN OLD MOVIE DEPICTION of human loneliness might show a solitary man sitting alone in an empty bar saying, "Here it is Christmas and I'm all by myself!" Although Christians acknowledge Easter as the greater feast, Christmas arouses more feelings. And those feelings are ambivalent. They like Christmas and they don't like it. They get too depressed, and anxious, yet they still try to prepare for it, celebrate it, and involve themselves in it. What is this Christmas phenomenon?

Most of the Christmas songs, rituals, and feelings floating around are about closeness, peacefulness, and being loved. However, one of the major feelings beneath the surface at Christmas is a desire to go home again, to be at home. We arrange to call home or actually be in our own home, but something else is present as well. It's as if we remember some great home or paradise we once had, then lost, and forever yearn to return to again. Adults brush it off as sentimentality or memories of happy childhood days.

But isn't it more than that, this yearning for home? Did we actually lose a home or paradise before the beginning of childhood? Were we somewhere wonderful before? How could we sense that there is more, and how could this sense be so deeply embedded in us, unless we experienced it? The people who wrote Genesis thought about this, and had an answer. Thousands of years ago they wrote about a garden, or paradise, from which human beings were expelled. They had the same feeling.

The deep, powerful feelings of Christmas go back beyond toys and good times of childhood, for even in childhood we grew tired of our toys. It is our spiritual "inner home" we are looking for, our union with God. We lived there briefly as we started life. We were inwardly at home with the universe and life. Some spiritual writers call it a unitive state, a condition of union with the Creator and the created world. We felt a security, an at-oneness with everything. However, it was not a conscious unitive state. It was as if at the beginning we were at home but our fuzzy intellects didn't know it. We just experienced it, and it preceded consciousness. Now we faintly remember it.

We did not stay in that paradise, that comfortable, wonderful home. God calls us to grow and reach an even greater home. God calls us to become a conscious, unique individual who relates to others and creation. God's plan is not that we suck our thumbs and bask or vegetate in the comfort of early pleasantness. God calls us to a challenging endeavor superior to personal comfort—we are called to learn how to love. And love involves emptying ourselves for others rather than staying comfortable. So we leave the early home of self-centered comfort and begin relating to others, to parents, siblings, friends, spouse—and give ourselves to them.

But once we have experienced, even preconsciously, this satisfying union, this being at home with God and existence, we are never cured of it. No matter where we go in this world, or by whom we are loved, or how wealthy we become, we have a sense that there is still more. There seems to be another home. It keeps calling us to find it again. We are basically homesick people. Christmas reminds us of that fact.

If we don't know what's really going on within us, we can feel unduly depressed, disappointed, or shortchanged. We can easily think that everyone else is much happier than we are. But if we know what's going on within us, our unfulfilled feelings can encourage us to keep on the road that will eventually bring us home. For the true antidote for our ambiguous feelings is the spiritual meaning of Christmas. God came here to tell us about the real home of paradise yet to come, and how to get there. God said the road home is found in loving one another. If we can only learn to love, then, in the words of T. S. Eliot:

> We shall not cease from exploration
> And the end of all our exploring
> Will be to arrive where we started
> And know the place for the first time.

# Moving from Misery to Meaning in Midlife

CHILDREN LOVE BIRTHDAYS because it means they're growing up. Adults approach birthdays with less enthusiasm. We're glad to be alive, have our friends and family, appreciate what we've accomplished. But, as the years accumulate, the snickering intimations of mortality get louder. We become more aware of time, limitations, leavings, and especially the ultimate leaving, death. So, some people solve birthdays by downplaying, ignoring, or joking about them.

After about thirty-five or forty birthdays, adults begin going through an inner disruption that can last for years. For some it's even a time of crisis. The middle part of life is so critical for us because our whole life is coming more into focus. A human is really like a house built straddling two continental shelves or plates—the shelves are the material or outer life and the spiritual or inner life. When shelves in the earth shift, earthquakes happen. When human shelves shift, "personquakes" happen.

There comes a time in everyone's life when a shift starts occurring. It's a normal shift, the purpose of which is to cause us to look within. If we don't run away from it by overwork, drugs, or other attempts to repress it, this shift leads us to ask ourselves questions such as, "Who am I apart from the roles and jobs I have?" Midlife is a wonderful, though often painful, opportunity to reorient our personality and develop a better sense of self. Many of us discover that we have been living a certain "false self," or imitation life. We have been guided chiefly by money, pleasure, success, or the expectations of others, rather than by real choices of our own. We have been living mainly in the material, outer world, and not acknowledging the inner, spiritual world. When the inner life begins to make its presence felt and rubs against the outer world, that person-quake occurs, and life may feel as uneasy as a building in an earthquake. This is a likely time for some to assume that their discomfort is caused by their spouse or their job, so they seek to regain former feelings of security by getting a new spouse or another job. Yet this person-quake is life's way, God's way, of nudging us further into growth and a deeper awareness of our true selves.

As we age, many of us experience for the first time a need to gain a sense of our whole self, its movement and meaning, not just a part of it, or a role, or meeting someone else's expectations. Besides being a wife, a mother, a husband, a father, or a businessperson, who am I? This need is not just for intellectual reasons or for the sake of nostalgia; rather, as I live, I want to know and hold my whole self in my hands, to understand and be my real and best self.

Can many birthdays, a long life, lead toward a rich life rather than away from it? Can the person-quakes of middle life serve a good purpose? Can later years be as fulfilling as earlier years? I like the possibilities that Rabbi Abraham Heschel offered late in his life:

> May I suggest that man's potential for change and growth is much greater than we are willing to admit and that old age be regarded not as the age of stagnation but as *the age of opportunities for inner growth?* The old person must not be treated as a patient, nor regard his retirement as a prolonged state of resignation.
>
> The years of old age may enable us to attain the high values we failed to sense, the insights we have missed, the wisdom we ignored. They are indeed formative years, rich in possibilities to unlearn the follies of a lifetime, to see through inbred self-deceptions, to deepen understanding and compassion, to widen the horizon of honesty, to refine the sense of fairness.

If each of our birthdays finds us moving toward these goals, then they really will be "happy" birthdays.

# Why Me?

SOME YEARS AGO, my sister Joan had a sudden medical problem. Not too long afterward she was lying on a hospital cart awaiting a minor operation. She felt a little frightened, in pain, and sorry for herself. A friend of hers, a physician, walked by and was surprised to see her there. "Joan, what's wrong?" he asked. She explained. Then she asked that question we all ask many times in life. She said to him, "I was just lying here feeling a little down and wondering, 'Why me?'" Being a good friend of hers, and a humorous man, he was able to bring a smile to her face when he said, "Heck, Joan, a better question would be, 'Why not?'" They both laughed, then had a helpful talk. She's always remembered the truth her question revealed in his joking reply, "Why not?" So have I.

The younger we are, the larger our ego. Child psychologists tell us that as newborns we have the impression that we are the center of the universe. Everyone else is at first experienced as just an extension of ourselves. In adolescence we still feel indestructible, egocentric, and ready to take risks of all kinds because we think we'll never die.

Some subliminal conclusions that we maintain in varying degrees even as adults include the following:

- My life will always have a certain logical fairness.
- I have something particularly special about me; other people will get sick and have problems but I will not.
- I find it extremely difficult to imagine my own death; I feel I'll live here forever.
- If I get into any kind of serious difficulty, someone or something will always rescue me.

Many adults resent the reality of aging or being confined to bed for some reason, or finding that our mind is not as skillful and adroit as it used to be. Such things should not be happening to me, and so we ask, "Why me?"

I have often thought of that doctor's wise retort, "Why not?" If I begin to feel that I am a victim of the circumstances of life, I've been forced truthfully to ask myself many times: "Am I supposed to be exempt from the problems of life?" "Are hard times supposed to only affect others, but not me?" "If that's true, what reasons can I realistically give that I am above the nitty-gritty of life?" And when I ask myself honestly, I can see there are no good reasons. We all share the same humanness. We are all affected by our mortality and the apparent inconsistencies of life.

Asking ourselves "Why not?" shouldn't depress us, nor does it take away our problems. However, it might help us to see reality more clearly, and to accept it more humbly. Instead of seeing ourselves only as victims or as special people exempt from the problems of life, the question can encourage us to handle the problems that come our way and to find personal growth in struggling with them.

We believe we have a silent contract with the universe, or with God. The contract—entirely of our own making—states that if we try to live a good and decent life, we will be rewarded by a certain comfort, prosperity, and longevity. We feel that the contract is breached by God when something goes awry in our life. We feel that we have held up our end of the bargain, so why has God not held up the other end by preserving us from harm, suffering, or discomfort? "Why me?" we ask.

"Why" and "Why me?" are the most commonly asked questions of life, whether we ask them aloud or in the silence of our mind. We'll never have the complete answers in this life, for we're dealing sometimes with what looks like irrational chaos, at other times with mystery, and always with the Mysterious One who is forming us. It's only later that we'll see how it all adds up to some grand and glorious purpose for each of us.

# Visiting Rest Homes

AIRPORTS HAVE METAL detectors through which everyone must pass. Suppose every visitor to a rest home for the elderly went through a "thought and feeling detector." What would it read?

Certainly the feeling detector would sound many beeps indicating the presence of love and appreciation for the person one is visiting—a parent, a spouse, a grandparent, an aged aunt or uncle. It would show many visitors' hearts reliving memories and treasured scenes from years gone by.

But it would also detect a lot of soberness, sadness, and even fear in the visitors. Going into a rest home tugs at us. It's not our favorite place to go. It makes us wonder if we are looking at ourselves years from now. We hate being reminded of our mortality. So we are traumatized at the sight of feeble bodies, walkers, and wheelchairs. We wince at the smell of medicine and urine, the sound of incoherent words, cries for assistance, or nurses who talk down to their patients in tones we might expect to hear used with four-year-olds. A person needs a solid sense of self, a bigger picture of life, and maturity to visit and leave a rest home in a serene way. An even greater amount of these qualities is needed by the people who hope to work in rest homes successfully and happily.

Are there any positive aspects to visiting a rest home? Certainly. To perceive them we need to focus our attention on the elderly people living there, not just on our fears. Think of the accumulated experiences of any one or all of the people there—the problems they have worked through, their accomplishments in raising children or running a business. Envision some of the intangibles—the relationships built, the creativity expressed, the reservoir of sacrifices for others, the joys and sorrows that have coursed through those bodies and minds over all those years. Sometimes when I pass a very old, large tree I think of all the seasons, storms, world events, and human lives that venerable tree has witnessed. The same holds for that old lady sitting in a wheelchair, or that old man staring out the window. What have they seen in their lives, where have they been?

Rest homes are places where some of the most crucial work of life is being accomplished. What we see are bodies that are not very pretty, muted minds that wander off. But within themselves these people are being purified. They are engaged in a final growing process of exchanging the nonessential for the essential, trading illusions for reality, resolving a lifetime of hopes and fears. They are discovering priorities. Sometimes the last thing we learn is what to put first.

The most important thing happening in a rest home is that people are getting ready to be born. Just as a child reaches a stage in the womb when it needs to move on and be born to the next stage, so does an adult at the other end of life. A certain readiness to move on is slowly achieved. The German philosopher Friedrich Nietzsche said, "What has become perfect, all that is ripe—wants to die. All that is unripe wants to live. All that suffers wants to live, that it may become ripe and joyous and longing—longing for what is further, higher, brighter."

I have encountered very old people who seemed to be "ripe" and ready to die. Not because they were overmedicated or dazed, despairing or depressed, but because they seemed to realize that they had gone as far as they could go in their journey here, and were ready to move on to a final, higher fulfillment of life. They seemed to be experiencing a sense of earthly completeness. It was as if they were saying, "I've grown and become as much as I can here—now I'm ready for what's next." Those of us who are still unfinished hold on to life more tenaciously because we have much work to do within ourselves before we reach that sort of maturity and faith.

The people in rest homes still need us. They need our conversation—not baby talk—and a genuine listening ear. They need to be hugged and touched often and warmly; they need respect and understanding; and they especially need to know that they are loved. When we are old, we need very little, but we need that very little, very much.

# If
# Seeds
# Could
# Think

WHEN SPRING COMES, we yearn to be in touch with nature and earth rather than plastic and computers. Many of us take to our yards with seeds, tools, and a vision. We till the ground and plant the seeds while imagining blossoming flowers some months in the future.

Suppose those seeds we place in the ground had a mind of their own. Imagine they could feel and think. How would they react to their situation and all that happens to them in order to bloom? Through no choice of their own, they find themselves buried in darkness under cold, moist earth. Varying pressures are experienced. From outside, the soil cxerts pressure on them. And a pressure from within, a force inside the seed itself, makes it feel that it must burst forth from its hard protective shell.

When the pressure from within becomes uncontainable, the seed breaks open and becomes a fragile plant. It pushes upward. But this is not easy. The delicate plant must push against and through a density greater than itself. But the seed persists. A life force within it urges it on, on to an unseen destiny. Even when it finally breaks through the soil, the journey is still not over. The plant now must experience day and night, heat and cold, sunshine and rain.

If it could think, feel, and speak, how many times might the seed complain about its existence? In its journey from dry seed to full blossom, how many times might it cry out in frustration, suffering, or confusion? It would have good reason to ask: "What is going on? Why must I live in such an unpleasant situation? What is this feeling and pressure in me that upsets my comfort? Why must I break

97

open and lose my protective security, then stand here vulnerable in cold rainstorms and glaring sunlight? Where am I going? What's going to become of me? I think I'd rather stop; I'm not sure it's all worth it; I hurt too much."

The seed would have no idea of its future until it blossoms. Only when that inner force pries open the tight bud into a magnificent flower never seen before, only when it is blooming radiantly in the sunlight, does it know. Then, all that went before becomes understandable and worthwhile; for something to fulfill the purpose of its existence is the most satisfying experience in the world. Beauty and fulfillment are self-explanatory.

Whenever we enjoy the flowers in our yard as they struggle to grow and bloom, we might think of ourselves. We, too, have been planted on this earth amid pressures, uncomfortable circumstances, and trying conditions. We, too, feel a life force within urging us to crack open and grow, to keep going no matter what obstacles surround us. We ask the very same questions our developing seed might ask. Many times we question or resist the growing process by saying, "I think I'd rather stop; I'm not sure it's all worth it; I hurt too much." Like a plant, we are as yet unaware of our final blossoming.

The One who planted us is an expert gardener with a vision of us as fully blossomed at some future time. God nurtures and prunes us, fertilizes us with enough joy to keep us going, enough pressures to keep us growing. It is only when we finally and fully open ourselves here, or in a world yet to come, that we understand all that has gone before in our lives. Only when we stand radiant in the light of existence at the end of all our growing is everything obvious and self-explanatory. We will have fulfilled the reason for our existence and become a unique being never seen before. We will be as beautiful as we were meant to be when God first thought of us.

# Doing Away with Timothy McVeigh

"ANYONE WHO MAIMS another shall suffer the same injury in return: fracture for fracture, eye for eye, tooth for tooth; the injury inflicted is the injury to be suffered. . . . One who kills a human being shall be put to death." That's what the Bible says in the Book of Leviticus (24:19–21), and also in Exodus. It's called the Law of the Talion, for *talion* means "similar punishment."

Why all the fuss, then, about the death sentence given to Timothy McVeigh for his role in the Oklahoma City bombing in which 168 human beings were killed? If the Old Testament says he should be killed, why do some clergy and laity disagree and assert that he should be kept in prison for life with no parole? Why do some people think that we should reconsider the death penalty? Don't they know the satisfaction that comes from seeing loathsome people get what's coming to them? Don't they realize that if we don't kill people like McVeigh, others may imitate him? Killing someone is not only a deterrent, it is a talion, a similar punishment that is necessary to keep peace. Besides, it costs too much money to keep people in jail for a lifetime.

And aren't those objecting clergy and laity going against what God wants? Let's look at the reasoning behind their objection to capital punishment.

In primitive cultures, life was so cheap and vengeance so strong that people overreacted to violence. The sentiment was, "Injure my relative and I'll kill you; kill one of my friends, and we will kill your whole family and tribe." We see remnants of this tendency in cultures that still punish a thief by cutting

99

off his or her hand, and in very young children, who sometimes say with their actions, "Knock over my blocks and I'll clobber you!" This can be called the Primitive Level of ethics.

In a world operating on such an ethical level, it's no wonder God said, in Exodus and Leviticus, "Don't operate by overkill, don't overreact to injuries; restrain yourselves, only do back what has been done to you." God called us to a level higher than the Primitive Level, to the Talion Level, where punishment is given only in similar measure. It probably sounded crazy to people who found overkill quite effective.

That might have been the end of the story—the Law of the Talion. Then Jesus Christ stirred things up. In the New Testament we see that he understood the Talion Level. But that didn't stop him from saying:

> "You have heard that it was said, 'An eye for an eye and a tooth for a tooth.' But I say to you, Do not resist an evildoer. But if anyone strikes you on the right cheek, turn the other also. . . .
>
> "Love your enemies and pray for those who persecute you, so that you may be children of your Father in heaven; for he makes his sun rise on the evil and on the good, and sends rain on the righteous and on the unrighteous." (Matthew 5:38–45)

Saint Paul sets out more of this teaching: "Do not repay anyone evil for evil, but take thought for what is noble in the sight of all. . . . Beloved, never avenge yourselves, but leave room for the wrath of God; for it is written, 'Vengeance is mine, I will repay, says the Lord.' . . . Do not be overcome by evil, but overcome evil with good" (Romans 12:17–21).

That may sound awfully silly when we are feeling gut-wrenching rage. A woman related to some of the Oklahoma City bombing victims said on the news, "I would like to see Timothy McVeigh die slowly and painfully."

Perhaps we're not ready yet to hear what Jesus Christ said. The world is hard and cold, and the Talion Level seems to work quite effectively. Why listen to the higher call to replace the Talion Level with the Level of Love? It seems that clenched fists, lethal injections, and severe punishments are what we really need.

And yet . . . ? We can't forget the call of that person named Jesus who said, "Love one another." That call has a strange, compelling attraction. God knows what we need and hunger for. Such ideals are not to dismissed, but longed for.

# Becoming Mature

THE JEWISH TALMUD contains this insightful quote: "Every blade of grass has its angel that bends over it and whispers, 'grow, grow.'" That could be said of anything that lives— blades of grass, kittens, golden retrievers, humans. Growing is always harder than not growing, and it needs encouragement.

All living things have a path of development they must follow to reach completion. Neglect this, or become fixed at any place along the way, and development is stunted. The final goal is delayed or not reached. As a living thing reaches age-appropriate levels of development, we call it "mature." Final maturity is that stage in an organism's life when it reaches the goal of its development. We wince when someone accuses us of being immature. It implies that we have not reached a certain age-appropriate level of development, or have stopped along the way.

No one is born mature. We have to grow into it, develop it. There is no shortcut. Blades of grass, kittens, and golden retrievers have only one track, the physical or organic, on which to grow and become mature. In humans, however, maturity has a twofold meaning. We have two dimensions to our being, the physical dimension and the psychological, spiritual dimension. We must grow on both these tracks to become mature. We've all seen people whose body has become mature but whose psychological life remains immature. They may be forty-five years old physically, but they behave in their inner, psychological life as though they were fifteen.

The physical track grows and develops pretty much on its own, unless we deprive it of proper care. The psychological and spiritual track is harder to develop. It's the most ignored and demeaned. Bumper stickers carry the graffiti of our age. I have seen bumper stickers on the cars of proud parents saying, "My child is an honor student at Farkle High School." Soon stickers appeared on other cars saying, "My kid is a boxer, and he beat up your honor student." Personally, I don't care for either sticker because of the comparison it engenders among our young, but those two stickers do acknowledge the two tracks in human development. One celebrates the psychological track, the other, the physical.

Of the two, the psychological and spiritual track most needs its cheerleaders, its angels who bend over us and urge us to "grow, grow." Inner growth and development are reached only through a lengthy process of facing crises, overcoming obstacles, and taking risks. Yet these are the very things we find hardest about life. We shy away from the catalysts most conducive to growth. We choose various defenses to avoid them, or cry, "Get me out of here!" When they occur, we feel insecure, hurt, or conclude that they are useless to our greater good. These are the times we enjoy seeing ourselves as victims, or accuse God of not caring or of treating us harshly. We expect inner maturity to just happen or to come at a discount.

As we face our crises and problems in life, it might help to imagine the following picture. On the one hand, here we are praying earnestly to God to take away a problem so that we don't have to go through it or struggle with it. And at the same time, this angel of God praying earnestly for us to grow and deal with the problem as best we can, rather than hope that it will be taken away.

We live in an age that hopes to have a pill for everything problematic and a defensive numbness against every pain. What we need more often are angel cheerleaders urging us to "grow, grow!"

# Remember When People Sinned?

NOBODY SINS ANYMORE, notice that? Who ever says to himself or herself, "I have sinned; God forgive me"? We hesitate to say somebody else sinned lest we be judgmental, and we hesitate to admit we've sinned lest we sound too religious or old-fashioned. Except for a few older clergy or evangelists, the concept of sin has disappeared from our thinking. Instead of saying we've sinned, we excuse ourselves.

We explain our immoral choices or weaknesses by saying it's someone else's fault. We say we had a terrible childhood, came from a dysfunctional home, weren't loved by our parents, grew up in a bad neighborhood, were the victims of prejudice. We flee from all responsibility. We imply that our choices are actually caused by somebody else. "Excuse me" replaces "Forgive me."

It's strange that the notion of sin has evaporated in our society just at the time when there are so many traces of it everywhere. It's rare that Catholics go to "confession" anymore, or, as minister friends tell me, that members of their congregations seek advice to overcome some particular sin or weakness. Sin is just not there! So that must mean we live in a society where love and kindness are widespread; where corruption, greed, and materialism are gone; and where we all feel secure and free from the threat of violence. Sure!

Perhaps we think that sin is gone because we don't know how to consider the concept of sin in a contemporary way, or we can't bear to see ourselves as sinners. We are a people who hate having our choices restricted or morally bound.

How should we look at sin today? For many centuries, sin was looked upon chiefly in a legalistic way—as breaking one of God's laws. And these laws of God were considered similar to human laws. They were arbitrarily made, changeable, and written on a list somewhere. They were external or unrelated to ourselves and God. Breaking one of these laws had to do only with behavior, not the heart.

Today we should strive for a deeper understanding. Sin is not just like breaking a human or societal law on some list. Sin involves a disruption or straining of a relationship, a relationship between oneself and God. Relationships are not stagnant; relationships are living—they grow or die, get stronger or weaker. A married couple's relationship, for example, is growing or diminishing every day. It grows or diminishes because of the choices and decisions made affecting the person loved. Sin is about choices deliberately made that bring about alienation, choices that disregard the other party in a relationship. Sin affects sinners within and slowly changes them and their relationships.

Sin not only alienates us from God, it also alienates us from ourselves. It brings about a loss of integrity, a frustration of our growth, and a disturbance of our rapport with others. Sin reaches down into the inner being of the sinner and, in the Greek vocabulary of Saint Paul, becomes *sarx,* which can be understood as selfishness incarnate. By my sin I don't just "break a law," I say, "to heck with my relationship with God and others, I'm all that counts."

The point of seeing and admitting our sins is not to beat ourselves down or damage our self-esteem, but to humbly search for truth and wholeness. When spouses admit their sins against their relationship, it is for the purpose of forgiveness and moving on to an even deeper relationship. When a human who sins admits her or his sin against God, it's for the same reason—to be forgiven and move on to an even deeper relationship. Admitting sin when it is there is like being our own moral jury. Instead of acquitting ourselves, we look within and say, "I'm guilty!" Then we rely on the forgiveness of the One who loves us so much.

# Time!
# Thief
# or
# Benefactor?

TIME IS WHERE CREATURES live. Created beings, like you and me, have a beginning and an end. One day we begin existing and one day we will stop existing. In between, we live in this thing we call time, composed of minutes, hours, days, and years. Time is especially on our mind as we leave one year and move into another.

In the time between our birth and our death a lot is supposed to be going on within us. Development takes place. We are to grow and increasingly become all we can be. We are to move from potentiality to actuality, just as an acorn gradually grows and becomes an oak tree. Time allows this transition and growing up. Time allows creativity.

The time during which we live is for us to unfold. It is not just to vegetate, or sit like some earthly couch potato watching life go by. It is to be a period during which construction takes place and our potential is realized. Just as the acorn becomes an oak tree, we are to become a fully developed human through and through.

We might ask why God made us like acorns, needing to grow and become trees. Why didn't God make us trees right away? Why didn't God make us in our completed, fully grown state? Why go through this puzzling and laborious process of making our own selves? Why go the long route? Why didn't God create us at point $Z$ instead of at point $A$?

If God created us at point $Z$ instead of point $A$, we would not be human beings, but something else. Humans have intellect and will; we can know, think, and choose. We're equipped for a journey, able to read the maps of life, understand directions, and make choices. Because of this we can join with God in our creation, or opt out. Human beings, the philosopher Jean-Paul Sartre claimed, make themselves, create themselves, decide themselves, choose themselves. And the choosing takes place over and over again in time. The flow of time, and billions of situations calling for a choice, offer us opportunities to become more and fulfill our potential. In contrast, God *is,* God does not *become.* God is the same through all eternity. We are the ones called to become and move from lesser to greater, from the past to the future.

Time is not automatically creative so that all we have to do is sit tight and wait. Rather, as each day comes, it calls for us to get involved and choose how to use it, to make decisions between what is good, healthy, and constructive, and what is unhealthy, evil, and personally destructive. Time offers us the chance to be creative, to help create our authentic selves.

A birthday, an anniversary, or a new year reminds us of time and what we are becoming by living in time. These events are opportunities to ask ourselves questions such as: "What kind of person am I becoming?" "Where are my choices taking me and what are they making me?" "Am I growing from small self-centeredness toward a larger concern for others?" "Am I more concerned about what I am collecting outside myself than what I am becoming inside myself?" "Just as a healthy oak tree grew toward its full potential during this past year, did I?"

The lyrics of a song once referred to time as a thief who stole from us our youth, our looks, our mental sharpness, our zest, and finally our life. That's one way of looking at time. Doing so leads us to be defensive, cynical, and afraid of the future. It implies that the best was in the past; it glorifies acorns rather than oak trees. Perhaps we need a song that celebrates time not as a thief, but as a benefactor who gives us countless chances to live and love and become the most wonderful human we can become.

# What Happened to Kim?

KIM WAS BLESSED WITH wonderful parents. They were people with hearts that easily opened toward anyone in genuine need. She grew up seeing that, being taught that, and it took hold. She had just turned twenty-two and was approaching college graduation. Vibrant and alive, Kim kept a special spot in her heart for people who were hurting.

One night she was returning to her dorm as twilight ebbed and darkness arrived. She had a big test the next day. Several friends had joined her for supper in a favorite restaurant, but now it was time to get back to her room and down to work. As she walked quickly from the restaurant back to campus, she passed a small alley between two buildings. As she passed the alley, she heard a groan. Pausing momentarily, she peered into the shadows. Someone was lying on the ground. The person groaned again. She stepped into the shadows, stooped over, and asked, "Can I help you?" Those were her last words. A hand clasped over her mouth and darkness descended. Her body was found the next day.

With hindsight, we might say that Kim should not have stopped, or that she should have found a phone and called the police. Those who are streetwise, cynical, or jaded might say, "She should have just passed on; it was none of her business." There is a point to such advice for prudence. But Kim acted with a compassionate spontaneity. She perceived a fellow human who hurt, and she responded immediately.

Leaving aside our arguments for prudence, what happens to people like Kim? Did this young, caring, altruistic person just cease existing? Did her person containing that thoughtful mind, those exquisite feelings, and twenty-two years of memories just evaporate when she was tragically killed? She lost the rest of her life on this earth for trying to care; did she also lose out in the big picture of existence? Did she somehow gain more than she lost, or do love and compassion turn us into fools?

Those who celebrate the truest spiritual meaning of Easter answer these questions in the negative. We believe that Kim in no way came out the less for her caring. Love is stronger than death, and, according to our varying religious convictions, we believe that life still goes on. Those of us who are Christians believe that Jesus Christ taught this and demonstrated it. We believe that life continues not in a more puny, joyless way, but that we pass over into a life of an intensity and fullness we cannot even imagine. In fact, if we knew the ecstasy òf the future life of those who truly love, it would be hard to keep us here.

We cling to what we know, however; we doubt what we cannot experience. This world seems to be all there is. Yet deep within us we notice a hunger for more, much more. Even before the end of a full life, we recognize that we are made for more than is on the menu here. We hunger for greater love, deeper relationships, complete understanding, and to have it all without end. We desire intense life so badly and are disappointed so often that some of us settle for cynicism and say that we only "project our wish" into an afterlife we'll never have. It's an illusion, say the cynics, the pie in the sky that keeps us satisfied rather than despairing. To such people, Kim was very foolish, for she lost everything.

Those who believe in a Creator discover both that God has a strong love for us and that God's decisions are unchanging. Once God says "Yes" and calls us into existence, there can never be a change of mind that says "No!" Any of us who, like Kim, live a life of love and compassion never really die, nor can our love make us less. Rather, we become more like the God of love and discover that love is the key to life, that love is even stronger than death. For all who live and love and die, God shouts a resounding and eternal "Yes!" that sustains us in ecstatic existence forever.

# Examination of Conscience

AN EXAMINATION OF conscience means just what it says. It is an honest personal examination of behavior and how people have responded to the voice of God as spoken through their own conscience. Back when most Catholics still went to confession, an examination of conscience was made before entering the confessional. Usually a format such as the Ten Commandments was used, and for each commandment people asked themselves if they had broken it, how, and if there was genuine sorrow for having done so. Some people made a brief examination each night, reviewing the events of the day before going to sleep.

To some, writing about an examination of conscience might seem silly today. The impression pervades society that nothing is really my fault. I'm either a victim or a saint, never a sinner. When I sin today it's either the fault of my parents for not raising me perfectly, of my spouse for being so unreasonable and irritating, of the "system" that failed me, of other people who "made me" angry and do what I did, or even God, who didn't treat me right. Comedian Flip Wilson facetiously excused his behavior by saying, "The devil made me do it!"

There's something honest, dignified, and cathartic about owning up to both my sins and my virtues. There's a dignity in saying (and meaning), "I did it, I was wrong, and I'm sorry." That's called responsibility. Psychologically and spiritually, it's also the best hope for forgiveness, growth, and improvement, for once I really see my weaknesses and sins, there is usually a subtle urge toward wholeness that nudges me to rid myself of them.

What might a contemporary examination of conscience ask me if I used it to look into my soul? If it was based on the Ten Commandments, here are a few examples I might find in its pages. Try them on yourself as a personal examination:

- Has my faith grown and deepened as I've become an adult, or do I believe less, trust in God little, and worry more about my own control of life?
- Have I kept a childish faith that experiences God only as a set of rules rather than a loving Person? Is God for me just a Divine Pacifier who is there to give me what I want when I want it, rather than my Creator whose will I am to follow?
- Do I use God's values in making personal decisions in my work, business, school, and home—or do I rely only on the pragmatic values of the world?
- How do I relate to my parents? Have I been able to forgive them for not being perfect?
- Do I give my parents time, respect, and love? Do I still find the time for the visit, the telephone call, the words "I love you"?
- Am I a person filled with anger? Are most of my thoughts of a negative, vindictive, victimlike nature so that I feel that life has cheated me? What is the chief source of my anger?
- How many people have I helped today by a kind word, by listening, by a compliment or encouragement?
- Do my relationships suffer because of my busyness?
- Do I tell others I love them just so I can use or enjoy them?

The purpose of examining our conscience is not to load on guilt, but to accomplish three main goals: first, to recognize the truth about ourselves, the good and the bad; second, to be genuinely sorry and ask forgiveness when we see that we have chosen wrongly and hurt others or ourselves; and third, to grow, improve, and become more whole.

We were created with a deep sense of what a human is to be. An examination of conscience is a way to check and see if we're on the right road and heading in the right direction.

# If No Death, Then Boredom

PART OF THE REASON WE jog, exercise, watch what we eat, and go to doctors is to try to live here forever. Who wants to give up the known for the unknown? Who wants to leave people we love and the beauty that surrounds us for . . . what? Who wants to die?

Some years ago, I had a thought-provoking jolt when I studied the topic of death anxiety. Surprisingly, some positive results can come into our lives when the fact sinks in that we are really going to die someday.

In a study, psychologists concluded that if there were no death and we knew this everyday life is how it would be forever, and ever, and ever—and we could never leave this world by death—intense boredom would result. Life shrinks when death is denied. Sigmund Freud, for example, believed that the temporary nature of life increases our enthusiasm for it. Death reminds us that existence cannot be prolonged. When death is denied, said Freud, life becomes as shallow as flirtatious love, in which there are no expectations of consequences or commitment. Gold and diamonds are precious because their supply is limited. Part of life's preciousness comes from the fact that our years are limited.

Realizing that life is limited can act as a catalyst to plunge us into more authentic (not hedonistic) ways of living, and enhance our joy in the true living of life. The authentic ways of living are those for which we are made—loving our families and others, living in the present, appreciating little things like spring days, the wind in our hair, or the drops of rainwater running down the windowpanes. Recognizing that life is limited encourages us to live purposefully, to discover a task in life that has meaning for us, and to dedicate ourselves to life with a joie de vivre that is intense and good.

It amazes me that so many of us have developed an attitude that God is antithetical to life. We suppose the Author of Life wants it to be boring. It's a sad deception we play on ourselves to excuse us from really living. One of my favorite quotes of Jesus Christ is in John's Gospel: "'I came that they may have life, and have it abundantly'" (10:10). We usually think that God wants us to tiptoe through life, sidestepping all its joys and sorrows and playing it safe. We envision a bland God, who desires for us a bland life, then gives us a bland heaven. Could it not be that, by discovering the preciousness and beauty of life, we might discover how tremendous is its Maker?

When we come more deeply to realize that our lives are limited, wonderful things can happen. Psychotherapist Irvin D. Yalom speaks of some of the positive inner changes noted in the lives of people he studied who had terminal cancer. These inner changes could be characterized in no other way than as "personal growth." Here are the changes Yalom reports:

- A rearrangement of life's priorities: a trivializing of the trivial
- A sense of liberation: being able to choose not to do those things that they do not wish to do
- An enhanced sense of living in the immediate present, rather than postponing life until retirement or some other point in the future
- A vivid appreciation of the elemental facts of life: the changing seasons, the wind, falling leaves, the last Christmas, and so forth
- Deeper communication with loved ones than before the crisis
- Fewer interpersonal fears, less concern about rejection, greater willingness to take risks, than before the crisis

As we read that list, don't we wish we could be like that every day? Yet these qualities did not appear until these people discovered that they were soon to die. Suppose we could realize the preciousness of each day without the onslaught of a terminal disease? And suppose we laid aside all the petty, begrudging, trivial things we get so wrapped up in? Suppose we saw our family and friends in a new light—and all other people as well? Suppose . . . Suppose . . . Could that be what God had in mind all along?

112

# Autumn Leaves, Autumn Lives

FOR JUST A FEW WEEKS of the year, our world looks stunningly different. During most of the year the trees are either bare or green. But for a short time, autumn showcases them with vivid golds and reds, dark browns and yellows. We take trips just to "see the leaves." Their beauty beckons us to go out for a walk and experience their impact.

Leaves are the most beautiful at their finale, for they have fulfilled the reason for their existence. It's as if they're crowned and celebrated. They were taken for granted throughout the long summer, but come autumn we can't help being attracted to their presence.

It should be true of humans, too, that the seasons of our lives lead somewhere, toward a beauty, a completion, and a culmination when we have fulfilled the reason for our existence. "The reason for our existence"—just what is that? Leaves exist to collect nutrients, produce oxygen, and so on, to support the life of the tree and the environment. What is the reason for human existence? To collect a lot of money? To become a celebrity, gain power over others, or stay young-looking forever? To get a degree or become famous? What is that purpose which, if we attain it, means that we have fulfilled the reason for our existence, and if we miss it, that we have failed? The purpose of a knife is to cut, the purpose of a wristwatch is to keep time; what is the purpose of a human?

Psychologists say that we are here to develop from a state of self-centeredness to altruism, from being in orbit around only ourselves to going out of orbit and touching positively the lives of others. Spiritually, we say the same thing. We are here to learn how to love. Saint Paul made this point so eloquently in his letter to the early Christians in the town of Corinth. He told them that their lives would be only like sounding brass and tinkling cymbals unless they learned how to love, that even faith and good works meant nothing without love. An old, anonymous spiritual adage says, "When the evening of this life comes, we will all be judged on love." When we reach our final season, love is what will make us more beautiful than autumn leaves. Humans are made to be lovers.

The autumn colors come gradually, not all at once. That's also true of love. We start life with such a pull toward self-centeredness. An infant is the center of its world. When hungry, a baby cries out, expecting parents to respond. Concern for others is beyond the capability of an infant. We grow beyond infancy, of course, and over a lifetime, over many seasons, we learn to love. As we grow and develop psychologically and spiritually, we come to realize that others have needs and feelings, too. And if love begins, we freely choose to give of ourselves to another. And if those choices to give of ourselves to others go on and on, we slowly become what we are choosing—we become loving, successful human beings.

We don't have to have loving people pointed out to us. We instinctively recognize them, just as we readily notice the leaves of autumn. Loving people have a sense of trueness or authenticity about them. They don't point themselves out, they just are what they are.

Winter is a time of solitude, silhouettes, and shadows. Spring is young and free and joyful. Summer is mellow and carefree. But autumn is rich, ripe, and complete; it nostalgically looks back over all that's gone before and is glad. What a way to end the year, or a life!

# God's Time and Our Time

ON MANY OCCASIONS GOD seems not to be on time. We pray and ask for something, and nothing happens; we ask to be healed, and we remain sick; we pray for more money to pay bills, and nothing comes. A single mother came into an inheritance and could finally afford to buy a larger home for herself and her children—only it happened after they were grown. She wondered, "Why couldn't this have been fifteen or twenty years ago?" Too often God seems not to be on time.

Yet, maybe God keeps a different time! The ancient Greeks had two words for time, *chronos* and *kairos*. The distinction between the two is a good one to keep in mind. *Chronos* means time in a quantitative sense. It's the kind of time we can count and divide into minutes, days, and years. It's the kind of time we can calculate on our clocks and wristwatches, the kind we measure on our calendars and planners. It's the kind of time that's always running out on us. This is the kind of time with which we are most familiar. It's the kind we expect God to respond to.

*Kairos* was the other ancient Greek word for time. It means time in a qualitative sense—not the kind the clock and calendar measure. In fact, it is a time that can't be measured at all. It's the time that is characterized by what happens in it, by its appropriateness. It's the kind that is meant when we realize it's "time to grow up," "time to be more responsible and take the bull by the horns," or "time to apologize." *Kairos* is more important than *chronos* because it usually affects our lives the most and means that something is happening inside us.

When we pray and ask God for something, we usually operate on *chronos*-time.

115

We pray to be healed of an illness or to get rid of a problem, and we expect it to be accomplished today—or tomorrow at the latest. But perhaps we are not ready, in *chronos*-time, for what we are expecting from God. Perhaps God knows that a much more crucial good comes to us by waiting, struggling, asking, until the right *kairos*-time comes. The single mother who would have liked a bigger home when her children were young, coped with the smaller home and became a very patient, humble, accepting person. Not obtaining her wish in chronological time seems to have brought her to a *kairos*-time, a quality time of personal growth and maturity. Later in life we can often look back and see many occasions when it worked for our good not to get what we wanted.

We get impatient when things don't happen when we think they ought to. We feel ignored, mistreated, or even victimized when life does not happen the way we want, or when we want. We even conclude that God doesn't care about us and our problems. Such times are excellent opportunities to remember that God may not come when we want, but God will always be on time.

# Christmas: When Mystery Draws Near

*MYSTERY!*
We don't use that word anymore.
Could it be because we think we know it all?
Could it be because what we can't experience,
    we conclude doesn't exist?
Because what doesn't fit the measurements
       of our mind
    intimidates us?

Mystery!
It is something we get lost in,
    can't figure out,
      that exceeds our imagination.
It is something bigger than we are,
    not under our control.

Mystery!
We don't like it.
It makes us seem so small.
It escapes our manipulations and mastery.
We can't hold it, touch it, think it.
It is too beyond.

Christmas is a mystery
    because it celebrates the One who is
      mystery,
    the God far beyond our meager mind.
God is more unlike we think
    than like we think.
God is power with no limits,
    time with no past or future,
      love whose passion we could not bear.

Christmas mystery
    is difficult to celebrate
    because it is difficult to fathom.
It means the far-exceeding One of immense power
    sets aside that power and becomes vulnerable.
It means the One beyond the limits of time
    lives then loses yesterdays, and wonders about tomorrows.
It means the One of strong, compelling love
    has to attract only subtly by divine flirtations.

Christmas mystery attracts
    because we and our world are cold and cruel
        and hunger for more than this;
    because all that is here is not enough for us;
    because deep within, we are mysterious beings ourselves;
    but mostly because we yearn so much to be loved.

Mystery draws near at Christmas saying,
"I am here, very close to you.
I cross over the line of the unknowable
    to make myself more knowable to you.
I take off my power and put on your life
    so as to live exactly as you live.
I express my love calmly by understanding and forgiving,
    leaving you free to seek my beauty—or not.
Do not be afraid! Hold me in your arms like an infant
    and look down into the eyes of the mysterious God
    who loves you very much."

# The Precious "Now"

WE SWIM IN THIS THING called *time*. It's all around us. Whenever we begin a new year, have a birthday, or celebrate an anniversary, we think of time. Just what is it?

Some philosophers have described time as a flowing succession of "nows." What we call the "past" is really made up of nows that have come and gone. Nows that have yet to happen we call the "future." The only part of time that really exists for us is right now. Since you began reading this reflection, many nows have come and gone. One of the awesome aspects of God is that for God there is no past or future. All is now. We get existence bit by bit; God has it all at once. In the mind of God we are as much two weeks old as we are forty years old or ninety. That's hard to grasp because we're not God.

Once when I was speaking on this subject a man asked, "If God sees my whole life at once, then he knows what I'm going to do ahead of time; that means I'm not free and I have to do what God knows I'm going to do, right?" In response, I asked him this question: "God knows if in twenty years you're going to be rich or not, correct?" He agreed. So I asked, "Then why keep on working? Why invest? Why save?" He got the point. Although God knows how the man would choose, and in making his choices whether he would grow wealthy or not, he was still free to do the choosing. God urges, strengthens, even nudges us throughout life to make wise choices, but *we* actually decide. As we receive each now, our choices and our efforts fill them. Each of us determines how we will use our present moment, with what motive and attitude—even though God sees the picture as a whole.

Most of the time we worry about the past (which is gone), or the future (which is not here yet), and we miss the most important moment: right now. The crucial question about the now that comes to me each moment is, What do I choose to do with it and become by it? We become something—or I should say someone?—by the way we use our nows. We become richer or poorer, kinder or more cruel, loving or selfish, serene or angry. As we receive and fill the present moment and then let go of it, it leaves its mark on us. It does not just mark our body with evidence that it was here, but it especially affects our soul. We slowly become what we choose as we pass through the nows and they turn into days, weeks, and years. At the end, we are what we chose to become.

When I taught high school, my students and I had a great discussion one day. Many remarked how they found most adults to be negative, angry, always worrying, and apparently possessing little zest for life. "Adults frown a lot," someone said. "They seem to have lost the ability to enjoy the simple things of life."

To try to impart a little understanding for us frowning adults, I discussed the hardness of life, the responsibilities, the dashed hopes, and the mortality we start experiencing in our body. I reminded the students of lost opportunities, unrequited love, and the toll that illness takes. Yet I knew that my students were sending me a valid message across our difference in years. When we who are now adults sat in their desks, we felt as they did, more buoyant, spontaneous, and optimistic. We have changed with the years and lost some excellent qualities that we could have preserved and developed. When we were young, we, too, idealistically dreamed of how we would remain vibrant and change the world. However, we have found that it is a hard enough task just to keep the world from changing us for the worse.

One way for us to preserve that quality, whatever our age, is to ask ourselves: How am I using my nows? Do I have a cynical, angry, victimlike attitude as I possess my moments of life? Do I think the best is past? Am I aware that the now I have is the same now a child of two, a youth in high school, or a king has? Can I feel fortunate right now, appreciate the work I do, the people I know, the love I receive, the talents I have, the beauty of the earth? When I let go of this now, and receive the next one, what will I be? My thoughts influence my attitudes, my attitudes influence my state of being, my state of being becomes more and more me. Who am I becoming?

# Three Classes of People

THREE CLASSES OF PEOPLE exist in the world—those who make things happen, those who watch things happen, and those who wonder what happened. The second and third groups are by far the largest, and most of us belong to them.

In youth, we are committed to change and growth; we can't wait to grow up and become adults. We have dreams of what we could be, what the world could be, and we see ourselves playing a part in making it happen. For a while, most of us belong to the make-it-happen group.

But along the way, our exuberant desire for growth subsides. We prefer the security of the status quo, we hesitate to take risks, we doubt ourselves, and we let our dreams die. Maybe it's because we thought growing up and making it happen would be easy, fun, or automatic. However, we discover that growth occurs at a price. We must let loose of old ways and adopt new ones, leave familiar territory and step onto unfamiliar ground, relinquish the carefreeness of childhood and take on responsibility. We find that growth involves necessary losses, and losses hurt. We must lose the security of home and go off to school, lose the financial help we receive from our parents and get a job to provide for ourselves, lose the loving personal interest of a mother and father and go among strangers.

The difficulties and responsibilities of true growth lead many to conclude that we'd rather stop and stay where we are. It's easier, more comfortable. We forget that we are responsible for our growth, and think of it as something achieved by existing a certain number of years. When we lose interest in growth and a sense of responsibility for making it happen, we make the transition from the make-it-happen group to the watch-it-happen group. We become more passive and watch things happen to ourselves, our family, or our country. We conclude, "That's just the way it is."

Once we've joined the watch-it-happen group, we're pretty easy to spot. We display symptoms like watching television excessively, thriving on others' scandals, and leading lives lost in illusions. We get lost in soap operas, talk shows, listening in on scanners to the conversations of others. We opt out of being a participant in life and become an observer. We become "reactors" who only get involved when something touches our security or routine. We get quite disturbed if the electricity goes off so we can't watch our TV programs, but we rarely get disturbed at the banal content of those programs. We complain if the government becomes more restrictive, but do not write our congresspersons. Watch-it-happen people rarely vote or become politically active. We have minimal altruistic or caring involvement in life. We become eyes more than hands, ears more than heart.

If we ever become one of the third group that wonders what happened, we have really regressed on our path of growth. We have closed ourselves to life so much that we don't see cause and effect, the results of our daily choices, or even the direction in which we are heading. If we believe anymore in the necessity to keep growing, we don't know how to get there. When we're in the wonder-what-happened group, we are surprised when things happen to us that were no surprise to others; we walk down roads heading toward ruin, and are stunned when we get there. We lose touch. We are neither eyes nor hands, neither ears nor heart.

A few persevere in the first of the three classes of people, the group that makes things happen—happen within ourselves, for others, and for the world. In this group we have somehow kept alive many of the good motives that moved us early in life. We still have a dream that glistens on the other side of difficulties and obstacles, and a sense of responsibility that if we ever get there, it will be in great part due to our own efforts. So we "keep on keeping on." We keep on trying to grow when weariness says stop; we speak up or try to love when there hardly seems reason to do so; we search within ourselves rather than blame others. We have a vision. The name for the group that makes things happen is leaders. The world always needs them very much.

# The
# Capital
# Sins

IT'S HELPFUL TO BE ABLE TO name things, to put "handles" on them. That's especially true of our inner life. The more we mature, the more we wish to live purposefully, to know what we're feeling and why. So we seek names for our inner feelings, to organize our psychic world and give us insights. We learn that when we feel one particular way it is called "frustration," and another vague feeling is "awe," yet another is "sensuality," and so on.

We can name the tendencies in our moral life in a similar manner. From as early as the sixth or seventh century, humans began naming certain immoral tendencies as capital sins. The word *capital* came from the Latin *caput,* which means "head." The meaning of the word indicates that there are seven major sins that stand as the head and cause of all other sins. Their names are pride, envy, anger, lust, greed, gluttony, and sloth. Actually, it's more precise to think of them as certain dispositions toward sinning, tendencies in our character that threaten moral goodness.

The capital sins are depicted in various works of art and literature, such as Chaucer's *Canterbury Tales* and Dante's *Divine Comedy.* These tendencies are today as recognizable as they were centuries ago.

Pride is considered the strongest and most pervasive of all the capital sins. Pride is self-love gone awry, the tendency to make ourselves our own law, our own judge, our own morality, our own god. In the Book of Genesis, the primary deception offered to humans by the tempter in the Eden story was that in return for ignoring God, we could be as gods.

Envy is sadness at the good others have, as if it is an affront to us. Envy hates to see others happy. Charm, beauty, love, possessions, good times, a happy family, and so on, are all perceived as having been stolen from us. Envy leads us to denigrate others who possess qualities, such as success, beauty, or talent, that we actually admire and desire for ourselves.

Anger is unreasonable hostility directed toward those who harm or threaten us. There is a just and reasonable anger that helps us protect ourselves and uphold goodness. The capital sin of anger is uncontrolled and unreasonable. It expresses itself in violence, vindictiveness, revenge, and a mania for getting even or punishing. It is related to some frustration of our ego. The more our pride infects our anger, the less willing we are genuinely to forgive others.

Lust is the unreasonable focus on sexuality and a misuse of others for our own gratification. A healthy, wholesome sexuality is permeated with love for the other. Lust, though it tries to disguise itself as love, is the exact opposite. Lust is the isolation of sex from genuine love. Lust is a shifting of the center of personality from the spirit to the flesh.

Greed is a consuming focus on, and preoccupation with, material possessions and money. When filled with greed, we consider our worth from the point of view of what we have, rather than what kind of person we are. Things and money become an obsession, filling most of our time, energy, and thoughts. When greed rules, we are often difficult to spiritualize because we become closed to others and the unseen world of faith.

Gluttony is the excessive love of eating and drinking, alcohol or drugs. It enslaves the soul to the body and leads to self-indulgence, a weakening of the will, and callousness toward others.

Sloth is the excessive avoidance of our responsibilities, duties, and personal development. In the physical realm it appears as laziness, procrastination, and indifference. In the spiritual realm it takes the form of distaste for spiritual realities and contempt for self-discipline. Sloth always seeks the easy way out, the way that requires the least effort and involvement of self. It stifles personal growth.

Among the capital sins, we all have our personal pets, the tendencies we find hardest to resist. Yet, resisting them, and encouraging the opposing virtues, helps our growth, character, and spiritual wholeness. In writing this, I recognized some of my pets. Maybe you saw some of yours, too!

# Do We Dare to Look Honestly Inside?

IT IS EXTREMELY NECESSARY that we plumb the depths of our person. Doing so teaches us so much, awakens us so much, guides us so much. Unfortunately, however, most of us live on the surface of our life, afraid of what we might find deep within. Although it is beyond recall, the part of us called the unconscious constantly affects our life. This is the place in our psyche where we put away (repress) the feelings and events that are either too truthful, too embarrassing, too frightening, or even so wonderful that acknowledging them will require us to live up to them. We have put them away so well that they are only coaxed out to consciousness gradually, or they pique our awareness in dreams, associations, or slips of the tongue. The hard work of seeking them out is called analysis. If we don't look deep, we never meet our real self.

Some years ago I spoke with a man who had the courage to take a peek inside himself and was amazed at what he saw. He was the father of several children. One of his boys was in college. The father came to me one day seething. He was enraged about this son. Dad had just discovered that his son had slept with several girls at college. The father sat there stewing. He said sternly: "I did not raise my boy, nor am I paying his tuition, so that he could be a low-life stud. I raised him to be a good Christian, to be responsible in all areas of life, including his sexuality." The most notable thing in our encounter was not what the father said, but how extremely angry he was.

On the surface he was a good father, worried over what he perceived to be his son's failing morals. And he had good reason

125

to be. I knew the dad and held him in high esteem, and was sorry to hear about the behavior of his son. But something about the intensity of his rage implied that his son's promiscuous actions touched on something deeper in the dad himself. Whenever we are extremely affected by things outside us, it is usually symptomatic of important things in our unconscious of which we are presently unaware.

We talked at length. We tried to look deeper. Before he left, he asked to come back in several days when he had cooled down. When he returned, his demeanor was completely different. He had discovered something about himself after much thought, something that was personally embarrassing but true. Yes, he was distressed at the promiscuous behavior of his son, and well he should be. None of us would want a child of ours to be so casual with something as sacred as human sexuality. But he had discovered a deeper reason for the strength of his rage. The father was envious! He came to see his own desire for the same promiscuity. He discovered in himself the wish that when he was in college he could have sexually enjoyed the young women to whom he felt attracted. But he had not done so. Now, deep down, he envied the apparent freedom his son seemed to have. On the surface he seemed to be an angry father who could never have done anything like his son had done. But after his honest look within, he saw his own human weakness and lust. He was embarrassed. He did not like what he saw in his son, or in himself.

My esteem for the dad grew. He had the courage to recognize the truth of his own sin and the reason for his rage at his son's. He saw that he needed to work continually to develop his own spiritual life, as well as to forgive his son and discuss with him their common weaknesses and how to control them.

Looking honestly within ourselves is one of the most courageous things we can do. Looking within, we face our own demons, fears, sins, and inadequacies. We see ourselves as we really are, creatures with a mixture of good and evil, doubt and faith, virtue and vice. People of strong character resist and struggle with their demons; people of lesser character befriend them. People of no character don't even look within to know what's there.

# Our Grieving for Not Being God

WE COME TO A POINT IN our life when we must accept the fact that we're not God. That sounds strange at first. We might say, "I've never for a moment thought I was God." Don't be so sure! Child psychologists beg to differ. They tell us about the feelings of omnipotence we all have when we begin life. We think the world is merely an extension of ourselves, and everyone, especially our parents, owes us whatever we want, when we want it. We think we can take risks without experiencing consequences, that our strength and health will always be there, and that life will be a charmed existence. We believe desired goals will come with little or no effort on our part. We feel entitled.

If our upbringing goes well, we start meeting optimal frustrations. These are small or great situations in which we are frustrated by the cold facts of life. "You can't play with that now, your sister had it first, so wait until she's finished." "No, you can't go out tonight, you have homework." "I know you would like to hit the ball as well as Mike does, but you need to practice a lot and see if that helps." We meet people we want as friends or as a spouse, but they don't want us. We study hard in school but barely pass. The longer we live, the more we see our grandiose dreams, expectations, and visions frustrated. We seem to get only a piece of them, if that. Behind all our frustrations is often a resentment or quiet rage that this shouldn't be happening to us. We cling tenaciously to the long-held conclusion that our will should always prevail, and what we decree must occur—just like God.

Midlife is really a hard time for would-be Gods. We look at ourselves not only in the bathroom mirror, but in our inner psychic

127

mirror, which reflects all we had hoped for and wanted to be. Wanting to be immortal and forever young, we are disappointed to see our body age. Wrinkles, aches, and illnesses seem like insults to a person who presumed that he or she would be eternally strong and healthy. In the psychic mirror of our inner life, we often feel less fulfilled than we thought we'd be, more limited, not loved enough, and troubled that we won't be here forever. It's hard to be a deposed god.

Depressing? It can be if we keep alive the illusion that we are God. For God doesn't age, lose great dreams, or miss opportunities. God just has to will things and they happen. God doesn't get arthritic joints or headaches, lose big deals to a rival, or find out one day that he needs glasses. God doesn't get retired from a job to make way for younger gods who seem better qualified. God doesn't have to even think about dying and leaving everything.

What's the answer? The old adage, "Be yourself, but be your *best* self!" As long as we yearn to be God, we'll be disappointed and frustrated. Someday, sit and quietly study your dog or cat, or a bird outside in the yard. That creature seems to have a contentment and self-possession in just being what it is. It's not frustrated because it does not yearn to be something more than the limited creature it is.

Being a limited human being isn't that bad. It can be a wonderful endeavor. To be human means to become more in touch with ourselves, to know truth, to have feelings, to become truly wise, to appreciate what it means to be alive, to play a part in improving the world by our creativity, to drink in the beauty and truth that surround us, to have deep and good relationships with others. It means to develop a relationship with the God who actually exists, and to discover that God loves us passionately, beyond our dreams. And most of all, being human means to realize that we do have the potential to become more like the God we've always envied, though in an unenviable way. Not through the omnipotent, powerful qualities that impress us so much, but by learning to give ourselves away to others, by nurturing a quality called love. That's what it is to be godlike. Any takers for that kind of godly job description? Or might that be what we're trying to avoid in the first place by striving for omnipotence?

# The Difference Between Pleasure and Joy

MOST OF US CONFUSE pleasure and joy. We think it's pleasure we're after, but what we seek most of all is joy. Pleasure is certainly wonderful and natural. It gives us a temporary lift, pleases one or more of our senses, and transports us out of the humdrum of life into a more agreeable state. But too many of us look for pleasure and think it will always be accompanied by joy. Not so.

Joy is not an act, like laughter, sex, or eating a delicious meal. Joy is a state of being, the delightful realization that we possess something that is good, true, or beautiful. Joy comes from an ability to enter deeply into life, recognize its priorities, and achieve those priorities to a significant degree. Joy usually belongs more to those who accept the scars of life than to those who try to avoid them.

To better understand the difference between pleasure and joy, it is helpful to note three big differences between them.

First, pleasure comes from *things* such as money, sex, food, applause, fame, and so on. Second, pleasure depends on things that are external to ourselves. It comes from outside us and is channeled through one or more of our five senses. Third, pleasure is temporary and limited. If we eat too much of a good thing we first feel pleasurable satisfaction, but excess causes discomfort or pain. Ending the source of pleasure is necessary in order to enjoy it again.

The characteristics of joy contrast with those of pleasure. First, joy comes from relationships with *people,* such as someone to love or who loves us—family, friends, children. People who constantly need *things* to make them happy exhibit one of the symptoms of a lack of joy. Second, joy comes from within us, not from without. It is the weather of our emotional universe, created by living well. Paradoxically, it grows within us when we forget our own ego and begin to think genuinely about the good of others. The virtues that underlie joy are often ridiculed in a hardened, cynical world. Third, joy is steady and lasting, not temporary. It can be possessed in adversity as well as prosperity. No one can take true joy away from us; there is no time limit on joy, no way of having too much of it. In fact, it usually deepens and intensifies.

Many attitudes in contemporary society work against joy. One enemy is merchandising, which keeps telling us we won't be happy unless we have the right things or the latest thing. Another enemy is the age-old influence of our ego. Egoism tells us we are entitled to everything we want, and that the world owes us the satisfaction of our whims and desires. The latest twist is the overemphasis on our rights. Once we become obsessed with whether we are getting our due, and whether we're happy, we find many reasons to conclude that we aren't. So we seek more, and grasp at pleasures to soothe our hurt ego. Yet no amount of pleasure can compensate for the absence of joy on the inside. Running down wrong roads never gets us to our destination. Pleasure is good, but joy is our calling. True joy is one of the infallible signs of right living.

Acknowledgments *(continued)*

The scriptural quotations on pages 16 and 44 are from the New Jerusalem Bible. Copyright © 1985 by Darton Longman and Todd, London, and Doubleday, a division of Bantam Doubleday Dell Publishing Group, New York.

The scriptural quotations on pages 26, 99, 100, and 112 are from the New Revised Standard Version of the Bible, copyright © 1989 by the Division of Christian Education of the National Council of the Churches of Christ in the United States of America.

The extract on page 8 is from *The Road Less Traveled and Beyond,* by M. Scott Peck (New York: Simon and Schuster, 1997), page 23. Copyright © 1997 by M. Scott Peck.

The extract on page 12 is from *Hondo, My Father,* by Becky Crouch Patterson (Austin, TX: Historical Publications, 1979), page 212. Copyright © 1979 by Becky Crouch Patterson.

The Shakespeare quotation on page 19 is from *Macbeth,* act 5, scene 5.

The quotation by President Bill Clinton on page 21 is from "Life on Mars," by Leon Jaroff, *Time,* 19 August 1996, page 60.

The quotation by Bill Broadway on page 21 is from "Mars Sets Off Secular Rumblings," *Washington Post,* 18 August 1996, page D10.

The quotation by a Carthusian monk on page 27 is cited from *Seeds of the Spirit: Wisdom of the Twentieth Century,* edited by Richard H. Bell with Barbara L. Battin (Louisville, KY: Westminster John Knox Press, 1995), pages 2–3. Copyright © 1995 by Richard H. Bell.

The extract on page 30 is from *The Content of Faith: The Best of Karl Rahner's Theological Writings,* by Karl Rahner, edited by Karl Lehmann and Albert Raffelt (New York: Crossroad, 1993), page 514. English translation copyright © by the Crossroad Publishing Company. Permission applied for.

The quotation on page 30 is by Alfred, Lord Tennyson, *Idylls of the King*, "The Passing of Arthur."

The quotations on pages 31 and 32 are from *The Individual and His Religion: A Psychological Interpretation,* by Gordon W. Allport (New York: Macmillan, 1960), pages 59 and 78. Copyright © 1950 by Macmillan Company.

The Julien Green quote on page 39 is from *Credo,* by Louis Evely, translated by Rosemary Sheed (Notre Dame, IN: Fides Publishers, 1967), page 132. Copyright © 1967 by Sheed and Ward.

The quote by Saint Irenaeus on page 39 is cited from *Fully Human, Fully Alive: A New Life Through a New Vision,* by John Powell, SJ (Niles, IL: Argus Communications, 1976), page 7. Copyright © 1976 by Argus Communications.

The quotation on page 41 is from *Awareness: A de Mello Spirituality Conference in His Own Words,* by Anthony de Mello, SJ, edited by J. Francis Stroud, SJ (New York: Doubleday, 1990), page 4. Copyright © 1990 by the Center for Spiritual Exchange.

The quotation on page 59 is from *A Farewell to Arms,* by Ernest Hemingway (New York: Simon and Schuster, 1995), page 249. Copyright © 1957 by Ernest Hemingway.

The quotation on page 72 is from *Confessions,* by Saint Augustine, translated by Henry Chadwick (Oxford: Oxford University Press, 1991), page 3. Copyright © 1991 by Henry Chadwick.

The poem on page 90 is from *Four Quartets,* by T. S. Eliot (New York: Harcourt Brace Jovanovich, 1971), page 59. Copyright © 1971 by Esme Valerie Eliot. Used by permission of Harcourt Brace and Company.

The quotation on page 92 is from *The Insecurity of Freedom,* by Abraham Joshua Heschel (New York: Schocken Books, 1972), page 78. Copyright © 1966 by Abraham Joshua Heschel, renewed 1994 by Sylvia Heschel. Reprinted by permission of Farrar, Straus & Giroux.

The Nietzsche quote on page 96 and the extract on page 112 are from *Existential Psychotherapy,* by Irvin D. Yalom (New York: Basic Books, 1980), pages 208 and 35. Copyright © 1980 by Yalom Family Trust. Reprinted by permission of Basic Books, a division of Harper-Collins Publishers.